Collision Course: Unraveling The Tenerife Airport Disaster

Oliver Lancaster

Published by Oliver Lancaster, 2023.

While every precaution has been taken in the preparation of this book, the publisher assumes no responsibility for errors or omissions, or for damages resulting from the use of the information contained herein.

COLLISION COURSE: UNRAVELING THE TENERIFE AIRPORT DISASTER

First edition. July 31, 2023.

Copyright © 2023 Oliver Lancaster.

ISBN: 979-8223394389

Written by Oliver Lancaster.

Also by Oliver Lancaster

Chernobyl: Unveiling the tragedy. A Comprehensive Account of the Nuclear Disaster

The Bhopal Gas Tragedy: Unraveling the Catastrophe of 1984

The Deepwater Horizon Oil Spill of 2010: A Disaster Unveiled

Fukushima Fallout: Unveiling the Truth behind the 2011 Nuclear Disaster

Minamata Disease: Poisoned Waters and the Battle for Justice (1932-1968)

Evil Women: Unmasking History's Most Notorious Women

Bundy The Dark Chronicles: America's Infamous Serial Killer

Dahmer The Dark Chronicles: America's Infamous Milwaukee Cannibal

Zodiac The Dark Chronicles: America's Infamous Cryptic Killer

Bigfoot: The Comprehensive Investigation into the Elusive Legend

Chasing Legends: The Truth behind the Chupacabra

Chasing Legends: The Truth behind the Loch Ness Monster

Aokigahara Forest: The Heartbreaking Secrets of Japan's Suicide Forest

The Amityville House: The Haunting Secrets of America's Most Infamous Residence

The Stanley Hotel: The Mystery of Colorado's Historic Landmark

The Tower of London: The Haunted Past and Secrets of Royal Ghosts

The Winchester Mystery House: The Riddle of Sarah Winchester's Mansion

Vanished Skies: The Mysterious Disappearance of Amelia Earhart

Vanishing Point: The Bermuda Triangle Exposed

Poveglia Island: Haunting Secrets of Italy's Most Terrifying Haunted Destination

Tracing Footsteps: The Mystery of Madeleine McCann

Inferno in the Sky: The Hindenburg Disaster

Challenger: Tragedy and Triumph - Unraveling the Space Shuttle Challenger Explosion

Collision Course: Unraveling The Tenerife Airport Disaster

Watch for more at https://tinyurl.com/olanc.

Sign up to my free newsletter to get updates on new releases, FREE teaser chapters to upcoming releases and FREE digital short stories.

Or visit https://tinyurl.com/olanc

I never spam and you can unsubscribe at any time.

OLIVER LANCASTER

Disclaimer

The information presented in this book, "Collision Course: Unraveling The Tenerife Airport Disaster," is based on factual research and historical accounts. The author and publisher are not liable for any errors, omissions, or inaccuracies in the content. This book is intended for informative purposes only and should not be considered a substitute for professional aviation or legal advice. Readers are encouraged to verify facts and consult relevant experts for the latest information.

Collision Course: Unraveling The Tenerife Airport Disaster

OLIVER LANCASTER

Chapter 1: Introduction

The Tenerife Airport Disaster, which occurred on March 27, 1977, stands as one of the most tragic and deadliest aviation accidents in history. The catastrophe unfolded at Los Rodeos Airport, now known as Tenerife North Airport, situated on the Spanish island of Tenerife in the Canary Islands. This incident forever changed the way aviation safety procedures were developed and implemented, leaving an indelible mark on the aviation industry.

On that fateful day, two fully loaded Boeing 747 jumbo jets, operated by two prominent airlines, KLM and Pan American World Airways (Pan Am), collided on the fog-covered runway, resulting in the loss of 583 lives and leaving only 61 survivors. The sheer magnitude of the disaster and its heartbreaking consequences sent shockwaves through the global aviation community, leading to extensive investigations and a reevaluation of safety protocols.

The incident has been a subject of in-depth analysis and study for decades, and its lessons continue to resonate with aviation professionals to this day. To fully comprehend the events that led to the Tenerife Airport Disaster, one must delve into the sequence of events that culminated in this catastrophic collision.

The seeds of this tragedy were sown by a confluence of factors, starting with adverse weather conditions that shrouded the airport in thick fog, significantly reducing visibility. The unexpected fog had engulfed the island due to an unusual weather phenomenon known as the sea of clouds. As the fog obscured the runways, pilots faced challenging circumstances while navigating their aircraft.

Additionally, the Tenerife Airport Disaster was exacerbated by a chain of miscommunications and misunderstandings between the flight crews, air traffic control, and ground personnel. Language barriers, differing communication protocols, and the pressure of maintaining tight schedules all contributed to the confusion and misinterpretation of crucial instructions.

The situation escalated when both aircraft were diverted to Los Rodeos Airport following a terrorist bombing at Gran Canaria Airport, their original destination. With limited parking spaces available at Los Rodeos, the ground staff had to manage an overcrowded tarmac, further adding to the chaos and confusion.

At the heart of this tragedy was a series of misjudgments, including the decision-making process of the KLM flight's captain, who initiated a takeoff without proper clearance from air traffic control. This action brought the KLM jet onto a collision course with the Pan Am aircraft, which was taxiing along the same runway in an attempt to exit it.

The culmination of these unfortunate events led to the two massive planes hurtling towards each other at high speeds, leaving the pilots with minimal time to react and avert the inevitable disaster. The resulting impact and subsequent fireball were catastrophic, leading to an unparalleled loss of life in the history of commercial aviation.

In the aftermath of the Tenerife Airport Disaster, investigators and industry experts thoroughly analyzed the incident, identifying numerous lessons and recommendations that could enhance aviation safety. These recommendations included improvements in communication procedures, language proficiency standards for aviation personnel, and the development of advanced ground and cockpit technologies to enhance situational awareness.

As we embark on an exploration of the Tenerife Airport Disaster, it is essential to approach this tragic event with reverence and a commitment to understanding the human and technical factors that contributed to this devastating accident. Through careful analysis, we hope to shed light on the valuable lessons learned from this disaster and the impact it has had on aviation safety practices across the globe.

Setting the Scene:

The year was 1977, a time when commercial aviation was experiencing unprecedented growth and international travel was becoming increasingly accessible to the masses. Against this backdrop of excitement and progress, tragedy struck at Los Rodeos Airport on the picturesque island of Tenerife in the Canary Islands, forever altering the course of aviation history.

Tenerife, known for its sunny weather and idyllic landscapes, was a popular destination for tourists from various corners of the world. On March 27, however, the island was gripped by a rare and unexpected phenomenon - a dense fog rolled in, enveloping the airport and surrounding areas in an impenetrable veil. The fog was so thick that visibility was reduced to mere meters, making flight operations treacherous and challenging.

Amidst this atmospheric chaos, two mighty giants of the sky, a KLM Boeing 747 and a Pan American World Airways (Pan Am) Boeing 747, were destined to cross paths at Los Rodeos Airport. Both aircraft were on intercontinental flights, filled with hundreds of passengers eager to reach their destinations. The KLM flight, captained by Veldhuyzen van Zanten, was en route to Amsterdam, while the Pan Am flight, under the command of Captain Victor Grubbs, was bound for Los Angeles.

Unbeknownst to the passengers and crews aboard these flights, their journey would culminate in an unimaginable catastrophe that would leave an indelible mark on aviation history. This tragedy, known as the Tenerife Airport Disaster, was about to unfold.

Earlier that day, a terrorist bombing at Gran Canaria Airport had forced both flights to divert to Los Rodeos. As the fog rolled in, the ground staff at Los Rodeos found themselves overwhelmed by the unexpected influx of aircraft. The available parking spaces rapidly filled up, leaving little room to accommodate the large jumbo jets.

Meanwhile, air traffic control was under immense pressure to manage the situation and ensure that flights could safely depart once visibility improved. Amidst the chaos, communications between the control tower, flight crews, and ground personnel became strained, further complicating an already dire situation.

As the fog persisted, the atmosphere at the airport was tense and uncertain. Passengers awaited updates, unaware of the perilous circumstances that lay ahead. The crews, too, faced mounting pressure to make timely decisions while grappling with the ambiguity caused by the limited visibility and chaotic conditions on the ground.

As conditions began to marginally improve, the KLM flight received clearance from air traffic control to taxi down the runway in preparation for takeoff. However, due to a misunderstanding and miscommunication, the clearance was not definitive, leading to confusion in the cockpit. At the same time, the Pan Am flight, still on the runway, awaited further instructions to exit the active runway and make way for the KLM aircraft.

The stage was now set for a heart-stopping collision that would shatter the world's confidence in aviation safety. As the KLM flight initiated its takeoff roll, it hurtled towards the Pan Am aircraft, which was still on the same runway. Despite desperate attempts by both flight crews to avert disaster, the colossal jets collided, resulting in a fiery inferno and unspeakable loss of life.

The magnitude of the tragedy was immediately apparent, and its impact on aviation safety was seismic. It served as a stark reminder of the complexities and risks inherent in commercial flight operations, prompting a comprehensive examination of procedures and practices throughout the industry.

The Tenerife Airport Disaster led to groundbreaking advancements in aviation safety protocols, communication standards, and the implementation of innovative technologies to prevent similar tragedies. As investigators combed through the wreckage and analyzed the chain of events that had unfolded, lessons were learned, and changes were made to ensure that such a catastrophic collision would never be repeated.

Today, the Tenerife Airport Disaster remains etched in the collective memory of the aviation community. It stands as a poignant reminder of the importance of diligence, clear communication, and unwavering commitment to safety in every aspect of flight operations. As we delve deeper into the events that transpired on that fateful day, we hope to honor the memories of those lost by understanding the critical lessons that have since shaped aviation safety, making air travel safer for all who take to the skies.

13

Chapter 2: Background of Tenerife Airport

Tenerife North Airport, formerly known as Los Rodeos Airport, holds a storied history that predates the tragic events of the Tenerife Airport Disaster in 1977. Situated on the island of Tenerife in the Canary Islands, Spain, this airport has played a pivotal role in connecting the archipelago to the rest of the world and facilitating tourism and trade in the region.

The airport's origins can be traced back to the 1930s when the Spanish Civil Aviation Authority recognized the need for an airfield on the island to accommodate the growing interest in aviation. In 1935, construction commenced on the Aeródromo de Los Rodeos, and two years later, the airport was officially inaugurated. The name "Los Rodeos" was derived from the local area where the airport was built.

During its early years, Los Rodeos Airport served as a crucial stopover point for transatlantic flights between Europe and South America. The airport's strategic location made it an ideal refueling station, bolstering its significance in the global aviation landscape.

As the aviation industry continued to evolve, so did the infrastructure at Los Rodeos Airport. In the 1960s and early 1970s, the airport underwent substantial expansions and upgrades to accommodate the increasing number of travelers. The development projects included the extension of runways, construction of additional terminal buildings, and the implementation of modern navigational aids.

On March 27, 1977, the airport's history took a tragic turn with the Tenerife Airport Disaster. The collision between the KLM and Pan Am Boeing 747s resulted in significant loss of life and drew international attention to the airport's operational challenges, especially during adverse weather conditions.

In the aftermath of the disaster, considerable efforts were made to enhance safety measures at Los Rodeos Airport and airports worldwide. The airport's name was later changed to Tenerife North Airport (Aeropuerto de Tenerife Norte) as part of the rebranding and modernization process.

Over the years, Tenerife North Airport has continued to grow and adapt to meet the demands of an ever-increasing number of tourists and travelers. Today, it stands as one of the busiest airports in the Canary Islands, handling both domestic and international flights. Its proximity to popular tourist destinations like Puerto de la Cruz and Santa Cruz de Tenerife contributes to its importance as a gateway to the island's attractions.

The airport's strategic significance extends beyond passenger travel. Tenerife North also serves as a crucial hub for inter-island flights within the Canary Islands archipelago. It plays a vital role in connecting Tenerife with the neighboring islands of Gran Canaria, Lanzarote, and Fuerteventura, facilitating seamless travel and transportation between the different parts of the region.

Throughout its history, Tenerife North Airport has continued to invest in infrastructure, technology, and safety measures to ensure smooth and secure operations. The airport's administration has focused on improving navigational aids, enhancing air traffic control systems, and expanding terminal facilities to accommodate the growing number of passengers and airlines.

Despite the tragic events of the Tenerife Airport Disaster, the airport's legacy is one of resilience, adaptability, and a commitment to improving aviation safety. As the years go by, Tenerife North Airport remains an essential link between Tenerife and the world, carrying the weight of history while looking forward to a future that prioritizes safety and efficient air travel for generations to come.

Tenerife North Airport, also known as Los Rodeos Airport, plays a critical role in aviation operations, not only within the Canary Islands but also in connecting the archipelago to international destinations. Over the years, the airport has evolved to become a strategic hub for both passenger and cargo flights, contributing significantly to the region's tourism, trade, and overall connectivity.

1. Regional Connectivity: Tenerife North Airport serves as a crucial link between the various islands that make up the Canary Islands. As one of the main airports on Tenerife, it facilitates a large number of inter-island flights, connecting

travelers and cargo to destinations such as Gran Canaria, Lanzarote, Fuerteventura, La Palma, and others. This role is instrumental in fostering economic ties and social interactions between the different islands, promoting a sense of unity among the archipelago's diverse communities.

2. Tourist Gateway: The airport acts as a gateway to the scenic and popular tourist destinations on Tenerife. Tourists from across the globe flock to the island to experience its stunning beaches, volcanic landscapes, and vibrant cultural heritage. Tenerife North Airport welcomes travelers eager to explore the northern regions of the island, including the historic capital city of Santa Cruz de Tenerife and the picturesque town of Puerto de la Cruz. Its convenient location ensures that visitors can quickly access these attractions upon arrival.

3. International Flights: In addition to serving as a regional hub, Tenerife North Airport facilitates international flights to various destinations in Europe and beyond. Airlines from different countries operate regular services, connecting the island to major cities like Madrid, Barcelona, London, Amsterdam, and many others. This international connectivity boosts tourism, trade, and business opportunities for both Tenerife and the Canary Islands as a whole.

4. Handling Cargo Operations: Beyond passenger travel, Tenerife North Airport handles significant cargo operations. As an important logistics center, it plays a key role in importing and exporting goods, supporting local industries, and meeting the demands of the island's growing economy. The airport's cargo facilities cater to various industries, including agriculture,

manufacturing, and retail, ensuring efficient movement of goods to and from Tenerife.

5. Emergency Diversions: Due to its strategic location in the Atlantic Ocean, Tenerife North Airport serves as a crucial alternative landing site for transatlantic flights in emergency situations. In cases of severe weather, mechanical issues, or other unforeseen circumstances, the airport can accommodate and support diverted flights, providing a safe haven for passengers and crew.

6. Focus on Safety: Following the Tenerife Airport Disaster in 1977, safety measures at Tenerife North Airport were significantly upgraded and continue to be a top priority. The airport adheres to stringent international aviation standards and invests in modern technologies, navigational aids, and training for staff to ensure the safe and efficient handling of flights.

7. Supporting Local Economy: The airport's presence has a profound impact on the local economy, creating jobs and generating revenue through various businesses and services operating within and around the airport. The hospitality industry, transportation services, retail outlets, and aviation-related businesses all benefit from the airport's operations.

Tenerife North Airport is a pivotal player in the aviation landscape of the Canary Islands, acting as a critical link between the islands, facilitating regional and international travel, supporting cargo operations, and contributing to the growth of the local economy. Its historical significance, coupled with a relentless focus on safety and efficient operations, solidifies its position as a key aviation asset, connecting Tenerife to the world and promoting prosperity in the region.

21

Chapter 3: The Canary Islands' Air Traffic Situation

A t the time of the Tenerife Airport Disaster in 1977, the Canary Islands, including Tenerife, were experiencing a surge in tourism and commercial aviation, making air traffic conditions increasingly complex. The islands' unique geographical location in the Atlantic Ocean presented both advantages and challenges for aviation operations. Several factors contributed to the air traffic conditions and challenges faced by the airports in the Canary Islands during that period:

1. Increasing Tourism: The Canary Islands had become a popular tourist destination, attracting travelers from various European countries. This surge in tourism led to a substantial increase in passenger traffic at the airports, including Tenerife North Airport (Los Rodeos) and Gran Canaria Airport (the original destination for the two involved flights).

2. Limited Airport Infrastructure: The rapid growth in air traffic was not always matched with adequate airport infrastructure. Many of the Canary Islands' airports, including Tenerife North Airport, were originally designed to cater to smaller aircraft and handle a lower volume of flights. The increased demand placed strain on the existing facilities, leading to challenges in managing large numbers of aircraft and passengers.

3. Adverse Weather Conditions: The Canary Islands are known for their favorable climate, but they can also experience sudden changes in weather, particularly in the mountainous areas. In the case of Tenerife, thick fog could descend rapidly, reducing visibility and disrupting flight operations. The unpredictable nature of the weather posed significant challenges for pilots, air traffic controllers, and airport personnel in ensuring safe takeoffs, landings, and ground operations.

4. Diversion of Flights: The terrorist bombing at Gran Canaria Airport forced multiple flights, including the KLM and Pan Am Boeing 747s, to divert to Tenerife North Airport. The unexpected influx of diverted aircraft created congestion and limited parking space at Los Rodeos, further complicating ground operations and increasing the risk of miscommunication and misunderstandings.

5. Language and Communication: Language barriers were a significant issue in the Canary Islands, where Spanish and English were the dominant languages used in aviation communications. During the Tenerife Airport Disaster, the language barrier added to the confusion between the KLM flight crew, Pan Am flight crew, and air traffic controllers, making it challenging to exchange crucial information effectively.

6. Limited Ground Radar: At the time, some of the Canary Islands' airports lacked sophisticated ground radar systems that could aid air traffic control during low visibility conditions. This deficiency made it more difficult to track aircraft on the

ground and in the vicinity of the airport, potentially increasing the risk of runway incursions and collisions.

7. Time Pressure: Due to the diversions and delays caused by the bombing at Gran Canaria Airport, both flight crews and air traffic controllers were under pressure to expedite operations and get flights back on schedule. Time pressure can lead to rushed decision-making and reduced situational awareness, potentially compromising safety protocols.

The culmination of these factors created a challenging air traffic environment at the Canary Islands' airports during the time of the disaster. The dense fog, communication difficulties, congested runways, and time-sensitive situation combined to create a perfect storm of circumstances that ultimately led to the tragic collision between the KLM and Pan Am aircraft at Tenerife North Airport. The lessons learned from this disaster have since driven significant improvements in aviation safety, including enhanced communication protocols, better weather forecasting, and the implementation of advanced technologies to mitigate the challenges faced by airports in the region.

The events leading up to the fateful day of the Tenerife Airport Disaster on March 27, 1977, were a culmination of various factors, each contributing to the tragic collision between the KLM and Pan Am Boeing 747s at Tenerife North Airport (Los Rodeos). Understanding these contributing factors is essential to comprehending the gravity of the disaster:

1. Terrorist Bombing at Gran Canaria Airport: The day began with an act of terrorism at Gran Canaria Airport, one of the

busiest airports in the Canary Islands. A bomb explosion by a separatist group forced multiple flights, including the KLM and Pan Am flights, to divert to the smaller Tenerife North Airport. This sudden influx of diverted flights put immense pressure on the airport's limited resources and created a chaotic situation.

2. Congested Parking and Limited Facilities: The diversion of multiple aircraft led to an overcrowded tarmac at Tenerife North Airport. Parking space was scarce, and the airport's facilities were ill-equipped to handle such a large number of aircraft and passengers. The ground staff faced challenges in managing the increased traffic, refueling aircraft, and coordinating departures.

3. Communication Challenges: Communication difficulties emerged due to language barriers between the air traffic controllers, who primarily spoke Spanish, and some of the flight crews, who were more proficient in English. This language barrier hindered clear and concise communication, potentially leading to misunderstandings and misinterpretations of critical instructions.

4. Foggy Weather Conditions: The Canary Islands are known for their generally favorable weather, but on the day of the disaster, a rare and unexpected weather phenomenon known as the "sea of clouds" brought dense fog to Tenerife North Airport. The thick fog significantly reduced visibility, making flight operations challenging and contributing to the overall confusion on the ground.

5. Taxing to the Active Runway: As the fog persisted, air traffic control instructed both the KLM and Pan Am flights to taxi along the same runway (Runway 30) to position themselves for departure. This decision, influenced by the limited parking space, meant that the Pan Am flight was still on the runway when the KLM flight was preparing to take off, setting the stage for a catastrophic collision.

6. Premature Takeoff Attempt: In a tragic sequence of events, the captain of the KLM flight, Jacob Veldhuyzen van Zanten, misinterpreted air traffic control's instructions and initiated the takeoff roll without obtaining formal clearance. The communication confusion surrounding the takeoff clearance request contributed to this premature action.

7. Delayed Clearance Confirmation: The Pan Am flight crew, under Captain Victor Grubbs, was still on the runway when the KLM aircraft began its takeoff. Air traffic control realized the impending collision and urgently tried to warn the KLM flight to abort the takeoff. Unfortunately, the message was delivered late, and there was insufficient time for the KLM flight to stop.

8. Collision and Aftermath: The KLM aircraft, attempting to take off, collided with the Pan Am aircraft at high speed, resulting in a devastating impact and a subsequent fireball. The crash claimed the lives of 583 people, making it the deadliest aviation accident in history.

The Tenerife Airport Disaster remains a stark reminder of the importance of effective communication, decision-making, and aviation safety protocols. The events leading up to that fateful day highlighted the necessity for improved procedures, advanced technologies, and comprehensive training for all aviation personnel to prevent similar tragedies from occurring in the future.

COLLISION COURSE: UNRAVELING THE TENERIFE AIRPORT DISASTER

Chapter 4: KLM Flight 4805 - A Fateful Decision

KLM Flight 4805 was the Boeing 747 involved in the catastrophic collision at Tenerife North Airport (Los Rodeos) on March 27, 1977. The flight, operated by KLM Royal Dutch Airlines, was a scheduled service departing from Amsterdam Schiphol Airport in the Netherlands to Las Palmas Airport on Gran Canaria, one of the Canary Islands in Spain. Due to the terrorist bombing at Gran Canaria Airport, Flight 4805 was diverted to Tenerife North Airport along with several other flights.

Flight Crew:

1. Captain Jacob Veldhuyzen van Zanten: Captain Veldhuyzen van Zanten, aged 50 at the time, was an experienced and highly regarded pilot with KLM. He had accumulated over 11,700 flight hours and was renowned for his expertise in the aviation industry. Captain van Zanten was a chief pilot and instructor for KLM, often featured in promotional materials and representing the airline at various events.

2. First Officer Klaas Meurs: First Officer Meurs, aged 42 at the time, was the co-pilot of Flight 4805. He had accumulated considerable flying experience and was a qualified pilot-in-command on the Boeing 747 aircraft. First Officer Meurs had been with KLM for several years and was considered a competent and skilled aviator.

Passengers:

KLM Flight 4805 was carrying a total of 234 passengers, including men, women, and children, from diverse backgrounds and nationalities. As the flight had been diverted due to the bombing at Gran Canaria Airport, many passengers were likely eager to reach their intended destination in Las Palmas or continue their journey to other parts of the world. Unfortunately, the tragic events that unfolded at Tenerife North Airport denied them that opportunity.

Events Leading to the Collision:

Upon arriving at Tenerife North Airport, Flight 4805 joined a crowded tarmac with several other diverted aircraft. The congestion caused by the sudden diversion of multiple flights added to the complexity of the ground operations and placed pressure on the flight crew and air traffic controllers to expedite the departure process.

As the fog rolled in and visibility reduced, Flight 4805 faced further delays and uncertainty. The air traffic control tower instructed the aircraft to taxi along the same runway (Runway 30) to position itself for takeoff, a common practice known as backtracking. However, a series of miscommunications, language barriers, and misunderstandings led to confusion between the flight crew and air traffic control.

Inexplicably, Captain Veldhuyzen van Zanten prematurely initiated the takeoff roll without receiving formal clearance from air traffic control. The co-pilot, First Officer Meurs, attempted to question the captain's actions, but the gravity of the situation led to a critical breakdown in communication.

Meanwhile, the Pan Am Flight 1736, a Boeing 747 taxiing in the opposite direction on the same runway, was still in the process of exiting the active runway when Flight 4805 began its takeoff attempt.

The collision was imminent, and air traffic control urgently tried to warn Flight 4805 to abort the takeoff, but the message was delivered too late. Within moments, the KLM aircraft crashed into the Pan Am aircraft, resulting in a catastrophic explosion and fire.

The impact of the collision claimed the lives of all 248 passengers and crew on board Flight 4805, making it one of the deadliest aviation accidents in history.

The investigation into the events leading up to the collision revealed a tragic chain of misunderstandings, miscommunications, and factors beyond the control of the flight crew. The disaster at Tenerife North Airport forever changed aviation safety practices, emphasizing the importance of clear communication, standardized procedures, and a culture that prioritizes safety above all else.

The decisions made by the KLM crew of Flight 4805 played a crucial role in the Tenerife Airport Disaster. While the disaster was the result of a chain of events and contributing factors, several specific decisions made by the KLM crew significantly contributed to the collision:

1. Premature Takeoff Attempt: One of the most critical decisions that led to the disaster was Captain Jacob Veldhuyzen van Zanten's decision to initiate the takeoff roll without obtaining formal clearance from air traffic control. The captain was eager to depart quickly, likely due to the delays caused by the diversion and the foggy weather conditions. However, taking off without proper clearance was a violation of aviation regulations and a breach of standard procedures.

2. Misinterpretation of Air Traffic Control Instructions: The KLM crew's misinterpretation of air traffic control's instructions and the confusion surrounding the takeoff clearance request added to the critical breakdown in communication. First Officer Klaas Meurs attempted to question the captain's actions, but the captain seemed convinced that they had been cleared to take off.

3. Failure to Abandon Takeoff Attempt: As the Pan Am aircraft, Flight 1736, was still on the runway in the process of exiting, the air traffic controllers urgently tried to warn Flight 4805 to abort the takeoff. However, the KLM crew either did not hear or misunderstood the warning, and the takeoff attempt was not abandoned in time.

4. Overconfidence and Pressure to Maintain Schedule: Captain Veldhuyzen van Zanten's reputation as an experienced and respected pilot might have contributed to an overconfident demeanor. Additionally, the pressure to adhere to the airline's schedule, coupled with the congested situation at the airport, might have influenced the captain's decision to expedite the departure.

5. Failure to Perform a 180-Degree Turn: As the situation rapidly escalated, the KLM crew had the option of performing a 180-degree turn to exit the active runway and avoid the collision. However, in the critical moments, the crew opted to continue the takeoff, believing they were cleared for departure.

The combination of these decisions led to the KLM aircraft hurtling down the runway on a collision course with the Pan Am aircraft. Tragically, the crew did not have sufficient time to react and avert the disaster, resulting in the catastrophic collision and loss of hundreds of lives.

It is crucial to note that the KLM crew's decisions were made in the context of adverse weather conditions, language barriers, time pressure, and a congested airport environment. However, aviation investigations and industry experts concluded that the crucial decision to take off without clearance and the misunderstanding of instructions were pivotal factors in the disaster.

The lessons learned from the Tenerife Airport Disaster have since led to significant improvements in aviation safety, including enhanced crew training, better communication protocols, standardized procedures, and a greater emphasis on teamwork and assertiveness in the cockpit. Today, aviation professionals are trained to prioritize safety above all else, ensuring that such tragic events are less likely to occur in the future.

Chapter 5: Pan Am Flight 1736 - The Ill-Fated Journey

Pan Am Flight 1736, the Boeing 747 involved in the Tenerife Airport Disaster on March 27, 1977, was a scheduled service operated by Pan American World Airways (Pan Am), one of the leading international airlines of the time. The flight was en route from Los Angeles International Airport (LAX) in the United States to Las Palmas Airport on Gran Canaria, one of the Canary Islands in Spain. However, due to a terrorist bombing at Gran Canaria Airport, the flight was diverted to Tenerife North Airport (Los Rodeos), along with several other flights.

Background of Pan Am Flight 1736:

1. Flight Crew:

- Captain Victor Grubbs: Captain Grubbs, aged 49 at the time, was the experienced and seasoned pilot in command of Flight 1736. With years of flying experience and an impeccable record, Captain Grubbs was well-regarded among his colleagues. He had been with Pan Am for over two decades and was known for his dedication to safety and professionalism.

- First Officer Robert Bragg: First Officer Bragg, aged 39 at the time, was the co-pilot of Flight 1736. He was an experienced aviator with significant flying hours under his belt. First Officer

Bragg's expertise and skills complemented Captain Grubbs, making them a well-qualified and capable flight crew.

2. Passengers:

Pan Am Flight 1736 was carrying a total of 380 passengers from diverse backgrounds and nationalities. The passengers consisted of a mix of tourists, business travelers, and individuals returning home or visiting loved ones. As the flight had been diverted due to the bombing at Gran Canaria Airport, many passengers were likely eager to reach their intended destination or make necessary connections for their onward journeys.

Events Leading to the Collision:

Upon arriving at Tenerife North Airport, Flight 1736 joined the crowded tarmac with several other diverted aircraft, including KLM Flight 4805. The congestion caused by the sudden diversion of multiple flights added to the complexity of the ground operations and created challenges for both the flight crew and air traffic controllers.

As thick fog enveloped the airport, visibility was severely reduced, leading to delays and uncertainty. Air traffic control instructed both Flight 1736 and the KLM flight to taxi along the same runway (Runway 30) to position themselves for takeoff, a common practice known as backtracking. The air traffic controllers were faced with the challenging task of coordinating multiple aircraft in low visibility conditions.

While Flight 1736 followed air traffic control's instructions and continued to taxi along the runway, the KLM crew initiated the takeoff roll without proper clearance, leading to the tragic collision with the Pan Am aircraft.

The impact of the collision resulted in a catastrophic explosion and fire, claiming the lives of all 335 passengers and crew on board Flight 1736.

The crew of Pan Am Flight 1736, like their counterparts on the KLM flight, faced numerous challenges that day, including adverse weather conditions, communication difficulties, and a congested airport environment. However, it is essential to acknowledge that the decisions made by the KLM crew, particularly the premature takeoff attempt without clearance, were pivotal factors that contributed to the disaster.

The Tenerife Airport Disaster remains a solemn reminder of the importance of clear communication, standardized procedures, and unwavering commitment to safety for all aviation professionals. The lessons learned from this tragedy have since led to significant advancements in aviation safety protocols and procedures, ensuring that the memories of those lost will forever inspire safer and more secure skies.

From Pan Am's perspective, the events leading up to the collision at Tenerife North Airport were marked by uncertainty, delays, and challenging operating conditions. Pan Am Flight 1736, a Boeing 747, had departed from Los Angeles International Airport (LAX) in the United States with Las Palmas Airport on Gran Canaria, one of the Canary Islands in Spain, as its intended destination.

As the flight approached the Canary Islands, the crew received information about the terrorist bombing at Gran Canaria Airport. Due to the airport's closure, Flight 1736, along with several other flights, was diverted to Tenerife North Airport (Los Rodeos), adding to the already congested situation at the smaller airport.

The key events from Pan Am's perspective leading up to the collision were as follows:

1. Diversion to Tenerife North Airport: The decision to divert Flight 1736 to Tenerife North Airport was not an expected development for the crew and passengers. The flight's original destination, Gran Canaria, was much closer to Tenerife, and the diversion meant additional flight time, fuel consumption, and the need to adapt to the new circumstances at Tenerife North.

2. Congested Airport Environment: Upon arriving at Tenerife North Airport, the crew of Flight 1736 found the tarmac crowded with several other diverted aircraft, including the KLM Flight 4805. The sudden influx of multiple aircraft taxed the airport's resources and created challenges for air traffic control and ground operations.

3. Adverse Weather Conditions: Thick fog had descended over Tenerife North Airport, significantly reducing visibility. The foggy conditions complicated flight operations and made taxiing, takeoff, and landing more difficult. The limited visibility added an extra layer of complexity to an already challenging situation.

4. Taxiing on the Runway: As instructed by air traffic control, Flight 1736 began taxiing along Runway 30 to position itself for departure. However, the crowded runway and foggy conditions may have heightened the crew's awareness of the potential hazards of sharing the same runway with other aircraft.

5. Collision Warning: As Flight 1736 continued its taxi, the crew likely became aware of the KLM aircraft, Flight 4805, initiating its takeoff attempt. Air traffic control urgently tried to warn Flight 1736 to abort its taxi and exit the runway to avoid a collision. However, in the critical moments, the warning may have been delivered too late to take evasive action.

Tragically, the collision between the KLM and Pan Am aircraft occurred as Flight 1736 was still on the runway. The impact resulted in a catastrophic explosion and fire, claiming the lives of all 335 passengers and crew on board Flight 1736.

Pan Am Flight 1736, like KLM Flight 4805, found itself entangled in a series of events that would lead to the deadliest aviation accident in history. The congestion, weather conditions, and communication challenges at Tenerife North Airport, coupled with the KLM crew's premature takeoff attempt, culminated in the devastating collision.

The disaster profoundly affected Pan Am and the aviation industry as a whole, leading to significant advancements in aviation safety protocols, communication procedures, and crew training to prevent such tragedies from occurring in the future. The memory of those lost on that fateful day continues to inspire continuous efforts to ensure the highest standards of safety in air travel.

COLLISION COURSE: UNRAVELING THE TENERIFE AIRPORT DISASTER

Chapter 6: Air Traffic Control Communication

The Tenerife Airport Disaster was, in part, attributed to a significant communication breakdown between the aircraft and the air traffic control tower at Tenerife North Airport. The dense fog and adverse weather conditions further exacerbated the challenges faced by both flight crews and air traffic controllers. Several factors contributed to the breakdown in communication:

1. Language Barrier: One of the primary factors was the language barrier between the air traffic controllers and some of the flight crews. The official language of aviation is English, and it is commonly used for communication between pilots and controllers worldwide. However, at Tenerife North Airport, Spanish was the predominant language used by the controllers. This presented difficulties for some flight crews, particularly those whose first language was not English, as they had to navigate communications in a language they might not have been entirely fluent in.

2. Congested Radio Frequencies: With multiple aircraft diverting to Tenerife North Airport due to the bombing at Gran Canaria Airport, the radio frequencies became congested. The high volume of communications created challenges for both pilots and controllers to transmit and receive messages efficiently. In the crucial moments leading up

to the collision, critical instructions or warnings may have been delayed or lost amidst the radio chatter.

3. Limited Ground Radar: Tenerife North Airport did not have advanced ground radar systems at the time. Ground radar is a valuable tool for air traffic controllers to track and monitor aircraft on the ground and in the airport vicinity. Without this technology, controllers had to rely heavily on verbal communications with flight crews to coordinate their movements on the taxiways and runways. The absence of ground radar made it more challenging to have real-time situational awareness of aircraft positions, especially in low visibility conditions.

4. High Workload for Air Traffic Controllers: The diversion of multiple flights to Tenerife North Airport placed a tremendous workload on the air traffic controllers. They had to manage a sudden influx of aircraft, coordinate ground movements, and provide clear instructions to flight crews while dealing with reduced visibility and challenging weather conditions. The high stress and workload might have contributed to potential lapses in communication or delays in transmitting critical information.

5. Time Pressure and Scheduling: Both flight crews and air traffic controllers were under time pressure to get the diverted flights back on schedule. The expectation to expedite operations, coupled with the congested airport and adverse weather, could have increased the likelihood of misunderstandings and miscommunications.

6. Confirmation Bias: Confirmation bias occurs when individuals interpret information in a way that confirms their pre-existing beliefs or expectations. In the case of KLM Flight 4805, the crew's eagerness to depart and the belief that they had received clearance to take off might have led them to interpret air traffic control's instructions in a way that aligned with their desired course of action. This cognitive bias might have influenced the crew's decision to proceed with the takeoff without proper clearance.

The investigation into the Tenerife Airport Disaster highlighted the critical role of effective communication in aviation safety. As a result of this tragedy, improvements were made to communication protocols, crew resource management, and language proficiency requirements for pilots and controllers. Today, the aviation industry places a strong emphasis on clear and concise communication, standardized phraseology, and the continuous improvement of safety procedures to prevent similar incidents in the future.

The Tenerife Airport Disaster was, to a significant extent, caused by language barriers, misunderstandings, and miscommunications between the flight crews and air traffic control. These communication challenges played a critical role in the tragic collision between KLM Flight 4805 and Pan Am Flight 1736 at Tenerife North Airport. The following factors contributed to the breakdown in communication:

1. Language Barrier: Language barriers were a primary issue at Tenerife North Airport during the time of the disaster. Spanish was the predominant language used by the air traffic

controllers, as it is the official language in Spain. However, English is the universally recognized language of aviation, and it is typically used for communication between pilots and controllers around the world. Some of the flight crews, particularly those from international airlines like KLM and Pan Am, were more proficient in English than Spanish.

2. Miscommunication of Takeoff Clearance: One of the most critical misunderstandings was related to the takeoff clearance for KLM Flight 4805. The flight crew requested and received clearance from the air traffic controller to taxi into position on the runway for departure. However, due to the language barrier and the controller's accent, the crew of Flight 4805 might not have fully understood or correctly interpreted the response. Instead of receiving clearance for takeoff, they likely interpreted the controller's response as confirmation to begin the takeoff roll, even though they did not have formal clearance.

3. Radio Chatter and Congestion: The diversion of multiple flights to Tenerife North Airport led to congestion on the radio frequencies. The high volume of radio communications created a challenging environment for pilots and controllers to effectively transmit and receive messages. In the critical moments leading up to the collision, critical instructions or warnings might have been delayed or lost amidst the radio chatter.

4. Time Pressure and Stress: The diversion of flights and the terrorist bombing at Gran Canaria Airport created time pressure for both flight crews and air traffic controllers. The

expectation to expedite operations and get the diverted flights back on schedule added stress to an already challenging situation. High levels of stress can impact communication and decision-making, leading to increased risks of misunderstandings.

5. Lack of Standardized Phraseology: While English is the standard language of aviation communication, the use of non-standard phraseology or unfamiliar accents could have contributed to misunderstandings. Air traffic controllers are trained to use standardized phraseology to ensure clear communication, but variations in accent or phrasing might have made certain instructions less comprehensible to flight crews.

6. Confirmation Bias: Confirmation bias occurs when individuals interpret information in a way that confirms their pre-existing beliefs or expectations. In the case of KLM Flight 4805, the crew's eagerness to depart and their belief that they had received clearance to take off might have led them to interpret air traffic control's instructions in a way that aligned with their desired course of action. This cognitive bias might have influenced the crew's decision to proceed with the takeoff without proper clearance.

The combination of language barriers, misunderstandings, and miscommunications created a complex and challenging communication environment at Tenerife North Airport on the day of the disaster. The tragic collision serves as a somber reminder of the critical importance of effective communication in aviation safety. As a result of this devastating event, significant improvements have been made to communication protocols, crew resource management, language proficiency requirements, and standardized phraseology in the aviation industry to enhance safety and prevent similar incidents from occurring in the future.

COLLISION COURSE: UNRAVELING THE TENERIFE AIRPORT DISASTER

Chapter 7: Runway Construction and Layout

The runway configuration at Tenerife North Airport (Los Rodeos) played a significant role in the collision between KLM Flight 4805 and Pan Am Flight 1736. The airport had a single primary runway, Runway 12/30, which ran approximately 3,100 meters (10,170 feet) in length. The specific runway configuration on the day of the disaster, coupled with the congested airport environment and reduced visibility due to thick fog, contributed to the tragic collision. Here's how:

1. Single Runway: Tenerife North Airport had only one primary runway, Runway 12/30. The lack of parallel runways meant that both departing and arriving aircraft had to use the same runway for takeoffs and landings. This configuration is known as a non-parallel (intersecting) runway layout. When an aircraft is departing, it must use a portion of the runway while other aircraft might still be using it for taxiing or landing, potentially leading to congestion and less efficient operations.

2. Backtracking Procedure: On the day of the disaster, several aircraft were diverted to Tenerife North Airport due to the terrorist bombing at Gran Canaria Airport. To accommodate the increased traffic and limited parking space, air traffic control instructed both KLM Flight 4805 and Pan Am Flight 1736 to taxi on the active runway (Runway 30) to reach their

designated positions for takeoff. This taxiing procedure is known as backtracking.

3. Congested Tarmac: The diversion of multiple aircraft to Tenerife North Airport led to a congested tarmac, with limited space available for parking and maneuvering. The backtracking procedure placed multiple aircraft on the runway simultaneously, including KLM Flight 4805 and Pan Am Flight 1736. This congestion added complexity to the ground operations and increased the potential for miscommunication or misunderstandings between the flight crews and air traffic controllers.

4. Foggy Weather Conditions: On the day of the disaster, thick fog enveloped Tenerife North Airport, significantly reducing visibility. The foggy conditions impaired the pilots' ability to see other aircraft on the runway or nearby, and it also made it more challenging for air traffic controllers to monitor the movement of aircraft visually. The limited visibility in combination with the congested tarmac created an environment where coordination and communication were even more critical.

5. Premature Takeoff Attempt: As KLM Flight 4805 was taxiing for departure, the flight crew misinterpreted air traffic control's instructions and prematurely initiated the takeoff roll without obtaining formal clearance. Simultaneously, Pan Am Flight 1736 was still on the runway, taxiing for its exit. This series of events led to a collision course, and despite air traffic control's urgent warnings to abort the takeoff, there was insufficient time for the KLM aircraft to stop.

COLLISION COURSE: UNRAVELING THE TENERIFE AIRPORT DISASTER

The non-parallel runway configuration, coupled with the congested tarmac, foggy weather conditions, and miscommunication, created a high-risk situation at Tenerife North Airport. The collision was a tragic consequence of a series of events and contributing factors, with the runway configuration and ground operations playing a crucial role. The disaster served as a stark reminder of the importance of effective communication, coordination, and situational awareness in aviation safety, leading to significant improvements in these areas in the aviation industry.

As of the time of the Tenerife Airport Disaster in 1977, Tenerife North Airport (Los Rodeos) was undergoing construction and expansion work to accommodate the increasing tourism and air traffic demands in the Canary Islands. The ongoing construction had a notable impact on the runway operations and the overall airport environment, potentially contributing to the complexities that led to the collision between KLM Flight 4805 and Pan Am Flight 1736.

The impact of ongoing construction on runway operations and safety included the following factors:

1. Limited Runway Availability: Construction work typically requires sections of the runway or taxiways to be closed or restricted, reducing the available operational space. The limited runway availability might have led to the need for backtracking, where aircraft were required to taxi along the active runway to position themselves for takeoff. This, in turn, increased the potential for congestion on the runway and

heightened the need for clear and effective communication between air traffic control and flight crews.

2. Temporary Taxiway Changes: Construction work could have necessitated temporary changes to the taxiway layout, which could have made taxiing procedures more complicated for both pilots and air traffic controllers. Pilots might have needed additional instructions to navigate through unfamiliar taxiway configurations, and air traffic controllers had to manage the flow of aircraft in the midst of changing taxiway routes.

3. Reduced Visibility and Hazards: Construction sites can create dust, debris, and other visual obstructions that could reduce visibility for pilots during taxiing and on the runway. The presence of construction equipment, vehicles, and personnel near the runway areas also increases the risk of foreign object debris (FOD) incidents, potentially posing hazards to aircraft during takeoff and landing.

4. Communication Challenges: Ongoing construction activities might have added to the complexity of radio communications between air traffic control and flight crews. Increased radio traffic related to construction operations could have contributed to congestion on the radio frequencies, making it more challenging for critical messages to be transmitted and received promptly.

5. Increased Air Traffic: As the Canary Islands were becoming a popular tourist destination, the ongoing construction at Tenerife North Airport might have attracted more flights, both

international and domestic. The increased air traffic, along with the diversions caused by the bombing at Gran Canaria Airport, placed additional stress on the airport's infrastructure, air traffic control, and ground operations.

It is essential to note that while the ongoing construction might have added to the complexities at Tenerife North Airport, it was just one of several contributing factors that led to the disaster. The collision was a culmination of a series of events, including foggy weather conditions, communication challenges, language barriers, and decisions made by the flight crews, particularly the premature takeoff attempt by the KLM crew.

Following the Tenerife Airport Disaster, aviation authorities and airport operators around the world emphasized the importance of safety during construction activities at airports. Today, rigorous safety protocols and procedures are in place to manage ongoing construction projects while ensuring minimal impact on runway operations and air traffic movements.

Chapter 8: Weather Conditions and Visibility

On the day of the Tenerife Airport Disaster, March 27, 1977, the weather conditions at Tenerife North Airport (Los Rodeos) were unusual and challenging. The Canary Islands, including Tenerife, are known for their generally favorable weather, making the conditions experienced on that day even more unexpected. The primary weather condition that significantly impacted the airport operations was dense fog.

Dense Fog:

The dense fog that enveloped Tenerife North Airport was caused by a rare meteorological phenomenon known as the "sea of clouds" or "whiteout fog." This type of fog occurs when warm, moist air from the surrounding ocean surfaces encounters cooler air over the elevated terrain of the island. The temperature inversion traps the moist air near the surface, leading to the formation of thick, low-lying clouds of fog.

The dense fog drastically reduced visibility to near zero on the runway and taxiways, creating an environment of low visibility. Pilots had difficulty seeing the runway markings and other aircraft, while air traffic controllers struggled to visually monitor the movement of aircraft on the ground. The combination of reduced visibility and the congested airport due to multiple diverted flights added to the complexity of airport operations.

The foggy conditions posed numerous challenges, including:

1. Reduced Visual Reference: Pilots rely on visual reference points during taxiing, takeoff, and landing. In dense fog, pilots lose visual cues and landmarks on the runway, making it difficult to maintain proper positioning and situational awareness.

2. Increased Reliance on Instruments: In low-visibility conditions, pilots must rely more heavily on their instruments for guidance during takeoff and landing. The transition from visual to instrument-based flying can be challenging, especially if pilots are not adequately trained or experienced in such conditions.

3. Communication Difficulties: The dense fog might have affected radio communication between air traffic control and flight crews due to the congestion on radio frequencies and potential signal disruptions.

4. Hazards of Ground Operations: The fog increased the risk of ground collisions and incursions, where aircraft or vehicles inadvertently enter a runway or taxiway without authorization. This is particularly concerning when the airport is dealing with a high number of diverted flights and a congested tarmac.

The combination of dense fog, limited visibility, and the airport's congested environment likely added to the already challenging situation at Tenerife North Airport on that fateful day. The adverse weather conditions, together with communication challenges, language barriers, and decisions made by the flight crews, contributed to the tragic collision between KLM Flight 4805 and Pan Am Flight 1736.

The Tenerife Airport Disaster remains a poignant reminder of the importance of effective communication, clear procedures, and the continuous prioritization of safety in aviation, particularly during adverse weather conditions. As a result of this tragedy, the aviation industry has placed a strong emphasis on improving weather forecasting, pilot training for low-visibility conditions, and airport infrastructure to enhance safety during challenging weather situations.

The dense fog that shrouded Tenerife North Airport (Los Rodeos) on the day of the disaster had a profound impact on visibility and flight operations, creating an environment of extremely challenging and hazardous conditions for both pilots and air traffic controllers. The reduced visibility and its effects on flight operations can be summarized as follows:

1. Near-Zero Visibility: The dense fog significantly reduced visibility to near-zero levels, making it extremely difficult for pilots to see runway markings, taxiway signs, and other aircraft on the ground. The lack of visibility prevented pilots from relying on visual cues and landmarks, a crucial aspect of safe navigation during taxiing, takeoff, and landing.

2. Disorientation: The low-lying fog created a "whiteout" effect, wherein the landscape appeared uniformly white, erasing any discernible horizon or visual reference points. This disorienting

phenomenon caused spatial disorientation for pilots, leading to a loss of situational awareness and making it challenging for them to accurately perceive their aircraft's position and orientation.

3. Instrument Flight Rules (IFR): The dense fog necessitated the activation of Instrument Flight Rules (IFR), which required pilots to rely primarily on the aircraft's instruments for navigation and flight control. Transitioning from visual flight to IFR can be mentally demanding for pilots, especially in high-stress situations, as it demands precise execution of instrument procedures.

4. Delayed Departures and Arrivals: The reduced visibility and the need for aircraft to adhere to IFR procedures led to significant delays in departures and arrivals. Pilots had to wait for the fog to dissipate or for visibility to improve before safely taxiing or taking off. This caused a backlog of flights and congested airspace, further complicating flight operations at the airport.

5. Ground Collisions and Incursions: With the dense fog limiting visibility on the ground, there was an increased risk of ground collisions and incursions. Pilots and ground personnel had difficulty visually identifying obstacles or other aircraft in their vicinity, raising the potential for accidents on the taxiways or runways.

6. Communication Difficulties: The foggy conditions and the diversion of multiple flights to Tenerife North Airport created congestion on the radio frequencies, leading to

communication difficulties between air traffic control and flight crews. Misunderstandings or delays in transmitting critical information could further complicate flight operations and coordination.

7. Heightened Stress and Pressure: The adverse weather conditions and the urgency to restore flight schedules placed significant stress and pressure on both flight crews and air traffic controllers. The high-stress environment could have affected decision-making and the ability to effectively manage the complexities of flight operations in challenging weather.

The dense fog, along with the other contributing factors to the disaster, culminated in the tragic collision between KLM Flight 4805 and Pan Am Flight 1736. The incident highlighted the critical importance of clear communication, standardized procedures, and comprehensive pilot training for adverse weather conditions. As a result of this disaster, the aviation industry has since implemented more robust weather forecasting, enhanced pilot training, and improved runway visibility technologies to mitigate the impact of adverse weather on flight operations and to ensure the safety of air travel in challenging conditions.

64

Chapter 9: Human Factors and Crew Resource Management

The Tenerife Airport Disaster was a tragic event that involved several human factors contributing to the collision between KLM Flight 4805 and Pan Am Flight 1736. These human factors played a significant role in the chain of events that led to the deadliest aviation accident in history. Some of the key human factors involved include:

1. Communication and Language Barriers: Communication breakdowns between the flight crews and air traffic control were critical in the disaster. Language barriers, specifically the difference in language proficiency and accents, hindered clear communication between the Dutch-speaking KLM crew and the Spanish-speaking air traffic controllers. Misunderstandings and misinterpretations of instructions occurred, leading to confusion and potential hazards.

2. Decision-Making Under Pressure: Both flight crews were under significant time pressure to depart Tenerife North Airport due to the congestion caused by the diversion of multiple flights and the urgent need to get passengers to their destinations. The pressure to maintain schedules and avoid further delays might have influenced the decision-making process of the flight crews, leading to a potential willingness to take more risks.

3. Confirmation Bias: Confirmation bias refers to the tendency of individuals to interpret information in a way that confirms their pre-existing beliefs or expectations. In the case of KLM Flight 4805, the captain's eagerness to depart, combined with the belief that they had received takeoff clearance, might have influenced the crew's interpretation of air traffic control's instructions to proceed with the takeoff.

4. Cockpit Culture and Hierarchy: The hierarchical nature of the cockpit, where the captain typically holds ultimate authority and decisions, might have played a role in the crew's reluctance to challenge the captain's actions. This cultural aspect of aviation could have hindered the first officer's assertiveness in questioning the captain's decision to initiate the takeoff without clearance.

5. Fatigue and Stress: Both flight crews were dealing with the stressful situation of being diverted to an unfamiliar airport, managing the needs and expectations of passengers, and handling the complexities of operating in low visibility conditions. Fatigue and stress can impact decision-making, cognitive abilities, and overall performance, potentially leading to errors and oversights.

6. Lack of Crew Resource Management (CRM): Crew Resource Management is a set of teamwork and communication principles designed to optimize flight crew performance and safety. At the time of the disaster, CRM was not as widely practiced and emphasized as it is today. Effective CRM training might have helped the flight crews navigate the challenging situation and prevent critical errors.

7. Training and Experience: The disaster highlighted the importance of training and experience in handling complex and unexpected situations. The flight crews' training in low-visibility operations and their experience in adverse weather conditions could have influenced their ability to manage the challenges at Tenerife North Airport effectively.

The Tenerife Airport Disaster serves as a poignant reminder of the impact of human factors on aviation safety. As a result of this tragedy, the aviation industry has made significant advancements in human factors training, communication protocols, crew resource management, and safety culture. The lessons learned from this disaster have led to lasting changes in aviation practices to prevent similar incidents and improve the safety of air travel worldwide.

Crew Resource Management (CRM) issues, fatigue, and decision-making errors were all significant human factors that contributed to the Tenerife Airport Disaster. These factors played a crucial role in the miscommunication and misjudgments that led to the tragic collision between KLM Flight 4805 and Pan Am Flight 1736. Let's explore each of these factors in detail:

1. Crew Resource Management (CRM) Issues:

CRM is a set of teamwork and communication principles designed to optimize flight crew performance and safety. In the context of the Tenerife Airport Disaster, several CRM issues contributed to the chain of events that led to the collision:

- Authority Gradient: The hierarchical nature of the cockpit, where the captain holds ultimate authority, can create an authority gradient that might inhibit effective communication and assertiveness from other crew members. The captain's decision to initiate the takeoff without clearance may have been influenced by the authority gradient, and the first officer might have been hesitant to challenge the captain's actions assertively.

- Communication Style: Communication between the flight crew and air traffic control is a critical aspect of CRM. Language barriers and differences in communication styles, compounded by the high workload and radio congestion, led to misunderstandings and confusion. Clear and assertive communication is essential in resolving conflicts and avoiding errors, but it was compromised in the challenging environment at Tenerife North Airport.

- Situational Awareness: CRM emphasizes the importance of maintaining situational awareness, especially in complex and rapidly changing situations. In the dense fog and congested airport environment, maintaining situational awareness became even more challenging for both flight crews. The crews' ability to perceive, comprehend, and project the evolving situation may have been hindered, impacting their decision-making.

2. Fatigue:

Fatigue is a significant human factor that can compromise cognitive abilities, decision-making, and overall performance.

COLLISION COURSE: UNRAVELING THE TENERIFE AIRPORT DISASTER

Both flight crews were likely fatigued due to the diversion and the associated stress of dealing with multiple logistical challenges, accommodating passengers, and navigating low-visibility operations. The impact of fatigue could have manifested in the following ways:

- Reduced Alertness: Fatigue can lead to reduced alertness and attention, making it more difficult for crew members to detect and respond to critical cues and warnings.

- Impaired Decision-Making: Fatigue can impair cognitive functions, including judgment and decision-making. The crews' ability to assess risks accurately and make prudent choices might have been compromised.

- Increased Error Proneness: Fatigue is known to increase the likelihood of errors, both in procedural tasks and communication. The combination of fatigue and the demanding environment at Tenerife North Airport could have led to critical errors.

3. Decision-Making Errors:

Several decision-making errors contributed to the disaster:

- Premature Takeoff Attempt: The most crucial decision-making error was the premature takeoff attempt by the KLM flight crew without obtaining proper clearance. The crew misinterpreted air traffic control's instructions, and their eagerness to depart influenced their decision to initiate the takeoff roll without formal clearance, despite not receiving a takeoff clearance.

- Failure to Abandon Takeoff: Once the KLM crew realized the potential conflict with the Pan Am aircraft, the decision to continue the takeoff rather than aborting it might have been influenced by the crew's belief that they had already been granted clearance.

- Confirmation Bias: The KLM captain's confirmation bias, where he interpreted the air traffic controller's ambiguous message as clearance to take off, likely contributed to the decision-making errors. The captain's strong belief in the accuracy of his own assumption influenced his actions.

The Tenerife Airport Disaster was a culmination of several human factors, including Crew Resource Management issues, fatigue, and decision-making errors. The language barriers, communication difficulties, high-stress environment, and decision-making under pressure created a complex and challenging situation for both flight crews and air traffic control. As a result of this tragedy, the aviation industry has made significant strides in enhancing CRM training, addressing fatigue management, and promoting a safety culture that encourages open communication and error prevention. These efforts are designed to prevent similar incidents and foster a safer aviation environment for passengers and crew worldwide.

COLLISION COURSE: UNRAVELING THE TENERIFE AIRPORT DISASTER

Chapter 10: The Collision and Immediate Aftermath

The collision that occurred at Tenerife North Airport on March 27, 1977, involved two Boeing 747 aircraft: KLM Flight 4805 and Pan Am Flight 1736. It remains the deadliest aviation accident in history. The collision was a result of a series of unfortunate events and human factors, with the dense fog and communication challenges at the airport playing a critical role.

As the day unfolded, Tenerife North Airport experienced an influx of diverted flights, including KLM Flight 4805 and Pan Am Flight 1736, due to the terrorist bombing at Gran Canaria Airport. The airport's limited capacity and the congested tarmac, combined with the dense fog reducing visibility to near zero, created a challenging operating environment for both flight crews and air traffic controllers.

The sequence of events leading to the collision was as follows:

1. Diversions and Congested Airport: Both KLM Flight 4805 and Pan Am Flight 1736 were diverted to Tenerife North Airport from their intended destination, Las Palmas Airport on Gran Canaria. This diversion was due to the bombing incident at Gran Canaria Airport. The sudden influx of multiple flights at Tenerife North Airport caused congestion on the tarmac, with aircraft parked in non-standard positions to accommodate the increased traffic.

2. Taxiing on Runway 30: After the diversions, the air traffic controllers instructed both KLM Flight 4805 and Pan Am Flight 1736 to taxi along the same active runway, Runway 30, to reach their respective positions for departure. This taxiing procedure, known as backtracking, required the aircraft to use a portion of the runway while other aircraft were still using it for taxiing or landing.

3. Communication Challenges: Due to the dense fog and the radio congestion caused by multiple diverted flights, communication between the flight crews and air traffic control was compromised. The language barriers and misunderstandings in the instructions and responses further added to the confusion.

4. Premature Takeoff Attempt: As KLM Flight 4805 taxied on Runway 30, the flight crew requested and received clearance from air traffic control to begin its takeoff roll. However, due to a combination of miscommunication and confirmation bias, the crew might have interpreted the controller's response as formal clearance to take off, despite not having received a takeoff clearance.

5. Pan Am Still on the Runway: As KLM Flight 4805 initiated its takeoff roll, Pan Am Flight 1736 was still on the same runway, taxiing for its exit. The dense fog and reduced visibility likely made it difficult for both flight crews to see each other's aircraft on the runway.

6. Urgent Warnings: Air traffic control urgently attempted to warn KLM Flight 4805 to abort its takeoff and to inform Pan

Am Flight 1736 of the KLM aircraft's position. However, the warnings might have been transmitted too late, and there was insufficient time for the KLM aircraft to stop.

7. Collision and Fire: Tragically, the collision occurred when the KLM aircraft collided with the Pan Am aircraft. The impact resulted in a catastrophic explosion and fire, leading to the loss of all 248 passengers and crew aboard the KLM flight and 335 passengers and crew aboard the Pan Am flight.

The collision at Tenerife North Airport was a devastating and complex accident that involved a combination of adverse weather conditions, communication challenges, human factors, and decision-making errors. This catastrophic event had a profound impact on aviation safety, leading to significant improvements in crew resource management, communication protocols, and training to prevent similar incidents in the future.

The immediate aftermath of the collision at Tenerife North Airport on March 27, 1977, was marked by utter devastation, chaos, and a massive rescue and recovery operation. The collision between KLM Flight 4805 and Pan Am Flight 1736 resulted in a catastrophic explosion and fire, causing the loss of 248 passengers and crew on the KLM flight and 335 passengers and crew on the Pan Am flight. The impact and ensuing fire caused extensive damage to both aircraft and created a scene of unimaginable tragedy.

Immediate Aftermath on KLM Flight 4805:

KLM Flight 4805, the aircraft initiating the takeoff, suffered severe damage from the collision. The impact caused a massive explosion and fire that engulfed the aircraft, leaving little chance of survival for those onboard. The cockpit area, where the flight crew was located, bore the brunt of the collision, resulting in instant fatalities for the crew members.

The rear section of the KLM aircraft, including the passenger cabin, also sustained significant damage from the impact and fire. The intense heat and smoke rendered escape nearly impossible for those seated in the rear of the aircraft. The rapid progression of the fire and the structural damage to the fuselage prevented any meaningful evacuation attempts.

Rescue and recovery teams rushed to the crash site, but the ferocity of the fire made immediate rescue efforts challenging. The rescue teams focused on extinguishing the flames and recovering the bodies of the victims. The wreckage of KLM Flight 4805 was left as a charred and twisted mass, a grim reminder of the tragic loss of life.

Immediate Aftermath on Pan Am Flight 1736:

Pan Am Flight 1736, the aircraft struck during taxiing, also suffered extensive damage from the collision and the subsequent fire. The area of impact on the Pan Am aircraft was its left engine and the lower fuselage, which resulted in a fuel-fed fire spreading through the aircraft.

The crash caused devastating casualties on Pan Am Flight 1736, with many passengers in the impacted area succumbing to the injuries and the fire. Some passengers seated away from the impact zone attempted to evacuate the aircraft, but the severity of the damage and the rapid spread of the fire posed formidable obstacles to their escape.

Like the KLM aircraft, the wreckage of Pan Am Flight 1736 became a site of immense tragedy. The rescue and recovery teams faced the daunting task of searching for survivors and recovering the bodies of victims amid the wreckage and the ongoing fire suppression efforts.

Impact on Tenerife North Airport:

The collision and subsequent fire caused significant disruption to airport operations at Tenerife North Airport. The airport's single runway, Runway 12/30, was closed following the collision, rendering the airport temporarily inoperable for flight operations. The diverted flights that had previously arrived at the airport were forced to find alternative landing sites, exacerbating the logistical challenges caused by the bomb attack at Gran Canaria Airport.

The airport's emergency services and personnel were immediately mobilized to respond to the disaster. Firefighting teams worked tirelessly to contain the fire and extinguish the flames, while medical teams provided emergency medical care to survivors and assisted in the recovery of the victims' bodies.

The aftermath of the collision saw the initiation of a thorough investigation to determine the cause of the tragedy and to identify lessons that could improve aviation safety. The collision at Tenerife North Airport remains a stark reminder of the importance of continuous efforts to enhance safety measures and prevent similar incidents in the future. The disaster had a profound impact on the aviation industry, leading to significant improvements in training, communication protocols, crew resource management, and air traffic control procedures to enhance safety worldwide.

79

Chapter 11: Rescue and Recovery Efforts

The rescue and recovery operations that followed the Tenerife Airport Disaster were massive, demanding, and marked by the dedication of emergency personnel, volunteers, and aviation professionals. The collision between KLM Flight 4805 and Pan Am Flight 1736 on March 27, 1977, resulted in a catastrophic explosion and fire, leading to the loss of 248 passengers and crew on the KLM flight and 335 passengers and crew on the Pan Am flight.

The immediate aftermath saw an urgent response to the disaster, focusing on rescue efforts, medical assistance, body recovery, and investigation. Here's a detailed account of the rescue and recovery operations:

1. Emergency Response Activation:

Immediately after the collision, emergency response procedures were activated at Tenerife North Airport. Airport firefighting and rescue teams, along with medical personnel, were dispatched to the crash site to respond to the unfolding disaster. Local emergency services were also mobilized to provide additional support.

2. Fire Suppression and Rescue Efforts:

The initial priority for the rescue teams was to suppress the flames and rescue any survivors. Firefighters battled the intense fire that engulfed both aircraft, spraying foam and water to control the blaze. However, the ferocity of the fire, combined with the severity of the impact, made it extremely difficult to access and rescue survivors.

3. Evacuation and Medical Assistance:

Passengers and crew who managed to escape the wreckage or were located away from the impact zones were provided with medical assistance. Ambulances transported the injured to nearby hospitals for treatment. However, the scale of the disaster and the extensive casualties overwhelmed the medical response teams.

4. Body Recovery:

Given the magnitude of the collision and the intensity of the fire, many of the victims' remains were severely damaged. Recovery teams faced a challenging and emotionally taxing task of searching through the wreckage to locate and recover the bodies of the deceased. The recovery efforts were slow and methodical to ensure that all victims were accounted for.

5. Site Investigation:

Concurrently with the rescue and recovery operations, an investigation team was deployed to the crash site to examine the wreckage and collect evidence. The investigation aimed to determine the cause of the collision and identify any contributing factors. The wreckage was documented, and crucial evidence, such as flight data recorders (black boxes), was recovered to aid in the investigation.

6. International Collaboration:

Given the international nature of the disaster, representatives from the Netherlands (KLM), the United States (Pan Am), and Spain collaborated in the rescue, recovery, and investigation efforts. The tragedy prompted a global response, with experts from multiple countries assisting in the recovery operations and accident investigation.

7. Psychological Support:

In addition to providing medical care, psychological support was extended to survivors, the families of the victims, and the rescue personnel. Trained counselors and mental health professionals were available to offer emotional support and counseling to those affected by the disaster.

The rescue and recovery operations at Tenerife North Airport were an arduous and emotionally draining process. The collision left a lasting impact on the aviation community, leading to significant improvements in safety measures, training, and protocols to prevent similar incidents in the future. The disaster served as a stark reminder of the critical importance of continuous efforts to enhance aviation safety and emergency response capabilities worldwide.

The Tenerife Airport Disaster was a catastrophic event that demanded heroic efforts from emergency responders, airport personnel, and volunteers who selflessly rushed to the scene to provide aid and support. In the immediate aftermath of the collision between KLM Flight 4805 and Pan Am Flight 1736 on March 27, 1977, these individuals displayed extraordinary courage, compassion, and dedication to help the victims and their families.

Their heroic efforts are a testament to the strength of the human spirit in the face of unimaginable tragedy. Here are some of the ways in which emergency responders and volunteers demonstrated heroism:

1. Firefighters and Rescue Teams:

The airport's firefighting and rescue teams were the first responders on the scene, facing intense flames and a chaotic environment. Despite the danger, they fearlessly battled the fire, spraying foam and water to control the blaze. Their quick response and bravery allowed them to reach the crash site swiftly and attempt to rescue survivors.

2. Medical Personnel:

Medical teams, including paramedics and doctors, rushed to provide medical assistance to survivors and treat the injured. These dedicated professionals worked tirelessly, administering first aid, stabilizing patients, and transporting the injured to nearby hospitals for further treatment. Their skills and quick action saved lives and provided comfort to those in need.

3. Search and Recovery Teams:

The search and recovery teams faced the grim task of locating and recovering the bodies of the deceased amid the wreckage and devastation. Their meticulous and emotionally taxing efforts ensured that all victims were treated with dignity and respect, and their remains were properly identified and handled.

4. Airport Staff and Volunteers:

The airport personnel and volunteers demonstrated extraordinary commitment in coordinating the emergency response efforts. They provided critical support, logistics, and communication assistance to the various agencies involved in the rescue and recovery operations. Despite the overwhelming circumstances, they remained steadfast in their commitment to helping those affected by the disaster.

5. International Collaboration:

Representatives from multiple countries, including the Netherlands, the United States, and Spain, collaborated in the rescue and recovery operations. This international cooperation showcased the unity of the global aviation community in the face of tragedy.

6. Psychological Support:

Trained counselors and mental health professionals offered psychological support and counseling to survivors, families of the victims, and rescue personnel. Their compassionate presence and understanding helped individuals cope with the trauma and grief they experienced.

7. Continuing Dedication:

The heroic efforts of emergency responders and volunteers did not end with the initial response. They continued to provide support and care during the investigation process and offered assistance to those affected by the disaster in the days, weeks, and months that followed.

The heroic actions of these emergency responders and volunteers in the aftermath of the Tenerife Airport Disaster exemplify the resilience and compassion of the human spirit. Their unwavering commitment to helping others in the face of great adversity serves as a powerful reminder of the importance of community, solidarity, and selflessness during times of crisis. The memory of their heroic efforts lives on as a tribute to those who lost their lives and a testament to the resilience of those who survived.

COLLISION COURSE: UNRAVELING THE TENERIFE AIRPORT DISASTER

Chapter 12: Investigation and Findings

The official investigation into the Tenerife Airport Disaster was conducted by the Spanish aviation authorities, specifically the Commission of Investigation of Civil Aviation Accidents (Comisión de Investigación de Accidentes de Aviación Civil or CIAIAC). The investigation aimed to determine the causes and contributing factors that led to the collision between KLM Flight 4805 and Pan Am Flight 1736 on March 27, 1977, at Tenerife North Airport (Los Rodeos) in the Canary Islands.

The investigation process was complex and extensive, involving a thorough examination of various aspects related to the accident. Some of the key areas investigated included:

1. Wreckage Examination: The wreckage of both KLM Flight 4805 and Pan Am Flight 1736 was extensively analyzed to reconstruct the sequence of events leading up to the collision. The examination included studying the aircraft structures, systems, and any evidence of mechanical failure.

2. Flight Data Recorders: The flight data recorders, commonly known as black boxes, from both aircraft were recovered and analyzed. The data from the recorders provided crucial information about the flight parameters, communications, and actions of the flight crews in the moments leading up to the collision.

3. Air Traffic Control Communications: The investigation examined the communications between the air traffic control tower and the flight crews of both KLM and Pan Am flights. The transcripts of radio communications were studied to understand the instructions given and the responses received.

4. Weather Conditions: The weather conditions at Tenerife North Airport at the time of the collision were carefully assessed. The investigation focused on the dense fog that reduced visibility and the potential impact of adverse weather on flight operations.

5. Human Factors: The investigation delved into human factors, including crew resource management, decision-making, communication, and the influence of fatigue on the flight crews' actions.

6. Airport Operations: The airport's operational procedures and infrastructure, including runway configurations, taxiway layouts, and any ongoing construction, were examined to identify any factors that might have contributed to the accident.

7. Timeline Reconstruction: The investigators reconstructed the timeline of events leading up to the collision based on available evidence, including radar data, communications, and eyewitness accounts.

The investigation team conducted interviews with surviving crew members, eyewitnesses, and air traffic controllers to gather firsthand accounts and insights into the events surrounding the collision.

COLLISION COURSE: UNRAVELING THE TENERIFE AIRPORT DISASTER

The final report of the official investigation was comprehensive and detailed, providing a thorough analysis of the accident's probable cause and contributing factors. The investigation concluded that the primary cause of the disaster was the combination of misunderstandings, miscommunications, and decisions made by the flight crews, particularly the premature takeoff attempt by the KLM crew without proper clearance.

As a result of the investigation, several safety recommendations were made to the aviation industry, focusing on improved communication protocols, crew resource management training, and enhanced procedures for dealing with adverse weather conditions. The lessons learned from the Tenerife Airport Disaster have had a lasting impact on aviation safety practices, helping to prevent similar incidents and improving the overall safety of air travel worldwide.

The key findings and recommendations stemming from the investigation into the Tenerife Airport Disaster have had a profound impact on aviation safety. The collision between KLM Flight 4805 and Pan Am Flight 1736 on March 27, 1977, resulted in significant loss of life and exposed critical safety deficiencies.

The findings and recommendations emphasized the importance of addressing human factors, communication protocols, crew resource management, and adverse weather conditions to enhance aviation safety. Here is an analysis of some of the key findings and recommendations:

Key Findings:

1.   Miscommunication and Language Barriers: The investigation identified miscommunication between the flight crews and air traffic control as a primary factor in the collision. Language barriers and differences in communication styles hindered clear and effective communication, leading to misunderstandings of instructions.

2. Decision-Making Errors: The premature takeoff attempt by KLM Flight 4805 without proper clearance was a significant decision-making error. Confirmation bias, combined with the pressure to maintain schedules, influenced the flight crew's judgment and contributed to the collision.

3. Crew Resource Management (CRM) Deficiencies: The investigation revealed deficiencies in CRM, with hierarchical cockpit culture potentially inhibiting open communication and assertiveness from the first officer in challenging the captain's decisions.

4. Adverse Weather Conditions: The dense fog at Tenerife North Airport severely reduced visibility and created a challenging environment for flight operations, contributing to the confusion and difficulty in managing aircraft movements on the ground.

Recommendations:

1. Improved Communication Protocols: The investigation recommended the development and implementation of standardized communication protocols between flight crews and air traffic control. This included clear and unambiguous

phraseology to minimize the risk of misunderstandings, especially in high-stress and congested situations.

2. Crew Resource Management Training: To address CRM deficiencies, the investigation called for enhanced CRM training for flight crews. The training focused on promoting assertiveness, effective communication, and the importance of teamwork to improve decision-making and situational awareness.

3. Standardized Checklists and Procedures: The use of standardized checklists and procedures was encouraged to minimize the risk of oversight and ensure that critical tasks were executed consistently during all phases of flight.

4. Enhancing Weather Forecasting and Reporting: The investigation recommended improvements in weather forecasting and reporting, especially at airports with unpredictable weather conditions. Timely and accurate weather information would enable flight crews to make informed decisions regarding operations in adverse weather.

5. Runway Safety Measures: To address runway incursions and collisions, the investigation recommended implementing runway safety measures, such as improved signage, lighting, and markings, to enhance ground operations safety.

6. Training for Low-Visibility Operations: The investigation called for specialized training for flight crews to handle low-visibility operations, including proper use of instrument flight rules (IFR) and techniques for taxiing in low visibility conditions.

7. Global Sharing of Safety Lessons: The findings and recommendations emphasized the importance of sharing safety lessons globally to prevent similar incidents and promote a culture of continuous improvement in aviation safety.

The impact of these findings and recommendations has been far-reaching, shaping the aviation industry's approach to safety training, communication protocols, crew resource management, and the management of adverse weather conditions. As a result, aviation safety has been significantly enhanced, and the lessons learned from the Tenerife Airport Disaster continue to be instrumental in preventing accidents and saving lives in the skies.

COLLISION COURSE: UNRAVELING THE TENERIFE AIRPORT DISASTER

Chapter 13: Impact on Aviation Industry

The Tenerife Airport Disaster had a profound impact on aviation regulations, procedures, and safety protocols worldwide. The collision between KLM Flight 4805 and Pan Am Flight 1736 on March 27, 1977, exposed critical safety deficiencies and prompted a reevaluation of aviation practices. As a result, several significant changes were implemented to enhance aviation safety and prevent similar incidents:

1. Standardized Phraseology and Communication Protocols: In response to the miscommunication and language barriers identified in the investigation, aviation authorities introduced standardized phraseology and communication protocols for air traffic controllers and flight crews. The use of clear and unambiguous language reduces the risk of misunderstandings during critical phases of flight.

2. Crew Resource Management (CRM) Training: The Tenerife Disaster highlighted the importance of effective teamwork, communication, and decision-making in the cockpit. CRM training became a standard practice for flight crews, emphasizing assertiveness, situational awareness, and the ability to manage complex and challenging situations as a team.

3. Enhanced Training for Adverse Weather Conditions: To address the challenges of adverse weather conditions, flight crews now receive specialized training in low-visibility

operations and instrument flight rules (IFR) procedures. This training equips pilots with the skills to operate safely in conditions with reduced visibility.

4. Runway Safety Improvements: To prevent runway incursions and collisions, airports have implemented runway safety improvements, such as enhanced signage, lighting, and markings. These measures help improve ground operations safety and reduce the risk of accidents on the runways and taxiways.

5. Improved Weather Forecasting and Reporting: The investigation underscored the importance of accurate and timely weather information. As a result, weather forecasting and reporting have been enhanced to provide flight crews with up-to-date and reliable data to make informed decisions about flight operations.

6. Implementation of TCAS (Traffic Collision Avoidance System): The Tenerife Airport Disaster led to the widespread adoption of TCAS, a technology that provides collision avoidance alerts to flight crews in the event of potential conflicts with other aircraft. TCAS has significantly improved the ability to detect and avoid mid-air collisions.

7. Global Safety Initiatives: The accident prompted the establishment of global safety initiatives, such as the International Civil Aviation Organization (ICAO) Universal Safety Oversight Audit Program, to assess and promote the safety oversight capabilities of civil aviation authorities worldwide.

8. Just Culture Approach: The disaster also influenced a shift in the aviation industry towards a "just culture" approach, where safety investigations focus on identifying systemic issues rather than placing blame on individuals. This approach encourages open reporting of safety concerns and fosters a culture of learning from mistakes.

9. Improved Accident Investigation Techniques: The investigation into the Tenerife Disaster also led to advancements in accident investigation techniques and technologies. Today, modern accident investigations use advanced tools, including flight data analysis and simulation, to reconstruct and analyze accidents more accurately.

The changes resulting from the Tenerife Airport Disaster have significantly improved aviation safety worldwide. The aviation industry's commitment to learning from past incidents and continuously improving safety protocols has led to a significant reduction in accidents and a safer environment for air travel. As a result, the lessons learned from the Tenerife Airport Disaster continue to shape aviation regulations and practices, ensuring that the tragedy's impact has led to lasting positive change in the industry.

Chapter 14: Lessons Learned and Training Improvements

The Tenerife Airport Disaster was a tragic and catastrophic event that resulted in the loss of 583 lives. This devastating collision between KLM Flight 4805 and Pan Am Flight 1736 on March 27, 1977, at Tenerife North Airport (Los Rodeos) in the Canary Islands has left lasting lessons for the aviation industry. These lessons have led to significant changes in aviation practices to improve safety and prevent similar incidents. Here are the key lessons learned from the Tenerife Airport Disaster:

1. Importance of Clear Communication: The disaster highlighted the critical need for clear and unambiguous communication between air traffic control and flight crews. Standardized phraseology and protocols were introduced to minimize misunderstandings and ensure effective communication during critical phases of flight.

2. Crew Resource Management (CRM) Training: The tragedy emphasized the importance of effective teamwork, communication, and decision-making in the cockpit. CRM training became an essential component of pilot education, promoting assertiveness, situational awareness, and the ability to work together as a team in challenging situations.

3. Safety Culture and Reporting: The accident underscored the importance of fostering a safety culture within the aviation

industry. Encouraging open reporting of safety concerns and incidents, without fear of punishment, helps identify potential hazards and improve safety practices.

4. Adverse Weather Preparedness: The dense fog and reduced visibility at Tenerife North Airport revealed the need for specialized training for flight crews to handle adverse weather conditions. Training in low-visibility operations and IFR procedures became standard to ensure safe flight operations in challenging weather.

5. Human Factors and Decision-Making: The disaster highlighted the influence of human factors on flight safety. Understanding how fatigue, stress, confirmation bias, and hierarchy can affect decision-making in the cockpit has led to improvements in training and safety protocols.

6. Runway Safety Enhancements: To prevent runway incursions and collisions, airports worldwide implemented runway safety improvements, such as enhanced signage, lighting, and markings.

7. Use of Technology for Collision Avoidance: The adoption of TCAS (Traffic Collision Avoidance System) and other collision avoidance technologies has significantly improved the detection and prevention of mid-air collisions.

8. Global Safety Initiatives: The tragedy spurred the establishment of global safety initiatives, such as the ICAO Universal Safety Oversight Audit Program, to enhance safety oversight capabilities of civil aviation authorities worldwide.

9. Continuous Learning and Improvement: The Tenerife Airport Disaster taught the aviation industry the importance of continuously learning from accidents and near-misses. This has led to ongoing improvements in safety regulations, practices, and technologies.

10. Just Culture Approach: The adoption of a "just culture" approach in safety investigations has fostered a more open and transparent reporting system, encouraging accountability for systemic issues rather than focusing on individual blame.

The Tenerife Airport Disaster served as a pivotal moment for the aviation industry, prompting significant changes in regulations, procedures, and safety protocols to prevent similar accidents. The lessons learned from this tragedy have been instrumental in improving aviation safety, making air travel one of the safest modes of transportation in the world. As the industry continues to learn and adapt, the memory of those lost in the Tenerife Disaster remains a powerful reminder of the ongoing commitment to enhancing aviation safety and preventing future tragedies.

The lessons learned from the Tenerife Airport Disaster have been incorporated into pilot training and air traffic control practices to enhance aviation safety. These implementations focus on improving communication, crew resource management, decision-making, adverse weather preparedness, and safety culture. Let's explore how these lessons have been applied in pilot training and air traffic control:

Pilot Training:

1. Crew Resource Management (CRM) Training: CRM training has become an integral part of pilot education, emphasizing effective teamwork, communication, and decision-making. Pilots are taught to work collaboratively in the cockpit, share responsibilities, and communicate clearly with other crew members, fostering a more open and proactive safety culture.

2. Standardized Communication Protocols: Pilot training now emphasizes the use of standardized phraseology and protocols during interactions with air traffic control. Pilots learn to communicate concisely, using clear and unambiguous language to minimize the risk of misunderstandings.

3. Adverse Weather Preparedness: Flight crews undergo specialized training to handle adverse weather conditions, including low-visibility operations and instrument flight rules (IFR) procedures. They are taught how to use onboard instruments effectively and navigate safely in challenging weather.

4. Human Factors Training: Pilots receive training on human factors and decision-making to recognize and mitigate the influence of fatigue, stress, confirmation bias, and other cognitive biases that may impact their performance.

5. Use of Collision Avoidance Technologies: Pilots are trained in the use of advanced collision avoidance technologies, such as TCAS, to help detect and avoid potential mid-air collisions.

Air Traffic Control:

COLLISION COURSE: UNRAVELING THE TENERIFE AIRPORT DISASTER

1. Improved Communication and Phraseology: Air traffic controllers receive training to use standardized phraseology and clear communication techniques to enhance interactions with flight crews. This training ensures that controllers provide concise and unambiguous instructions to pilots, reducing the risk of miscommunication.

2. Collaborative Decision-Making: Air traffic control training emphasizes collaborative decision-making and situational awareness. Controllers learn to work closely with pilots and share important information to support safe and efficient operations.

3. Managing Adverse Weather Conditions: Air traffic controllers are trained to handle adverse weather conditions and coordinate traffic flow during low-visibility operations. They must be prepared to adjust traffic patterns and provide accurate weather information to flight crews.

4. Safety Culture and Reporting: Air traffic controllers are encouraged to report safety concerns without fear of retribution. This fosters a culture of continuous improvement and enables the identification of potential hazards in the air traffic control system.

5. Advanced Systems and Tools: Air traffic controllers receive training on advanced air traffic management systems and technologies that assist in monitoring and managing air traffic flow more effectively.

The implementation of these lessons in pilot training and air traffic control has resulted in significant improvements in aviation safety. Airline crews and controllers now operate with a heightened awareness of the importance of effective communication, teamwork, and situational awareness. These practices have contributed to a decline in the number of accidents and incidents, making air travel safer for passengers and crew. Continuous learning and ongoing improvements in training and procedures ensure that the lessons from the Tenerife Airport Disaster continue to drive positive change and enhance safety in the aviation industry.

COLLISION COURSE: UNRAVELING THE TENERIFE AIRPORT DISASTER

Chapter 15: Personal Stories of Survivors and Families

The Tenerife Airport Disaster on March 27, 1977, left a lasting impact on the survivors and the families of the victims. The tragic collision between KLM Flight 4805 and Pan Am Flight 1736 at Tenerife North Airport (Los Rodeos) in the Canary Islands resulted in the loss of 583 lives, making it the deadliest aviation accident in history. The survivors and families of the victims were left to cope with the immense grief, trauma, and profound loss that followed the devastating accident.

1. Survivors:

The survivors of the Tenerife Airport Disaster faced the harrowing experience of escaping the burning wreckage and witnessing the tragic loss of so many lives. Many suffered physical injuries and emotional trauma from the ordeal. Some survivors struggled with survivor's guilt, grappling with why they survived while others perished.

Despite the challenges they faced, the survivors showed immense resilience and strength in rebuilding their lives. Many sought counseling and support to help them cope with the trauma and grief they experienced. Some survivors became advocates for aviation safety, sharing their stories to raise awareness about the importance of continuous improvement in safety protocols.

2. Families of Victims:

For the families of the victims, the aftermath of the Tenerife Disaster was a period of unimaginable grief and sorrow. They mourned the loss of loved ones, grappling with the sudden and tragic nature of the accident. Many families found comfort in coming together with other affected families, sharing their experiences and supporting each other in their grief.

The families of the victims sought answers about the cause of the accident and demanded accountability. Some embarked on a quest for justice, seeking legal action against the airlines and authorities involved. Others worked tirelessly to honor the memory of their loved ones, creating memorials and foundations dedicated to aviation safety and remembrance.

Over time, some families found solace in creating legacies for their lost loved ones through charitable initiatives, scholarships, or community projects. They turned their grief into action, working to prevent similar accidents and improve aviation safety to protect other travelers and their families.

3. Long-Term Impact:

The impact of the Tenerife Airport Disaster continues to reverberate through the lives of survivors and the families of victims. The memory of the tragic accident remains a part of their lives, forever shaping their perspectives and priorities.

In the years following the disaster, survivors and family members have advocated for improved aviation safety regulations, pushing for stricter adherence to safety protocols and enhanced training for flight crews and air traffic controllers.

The survivors and families of victims have also contributed to a global aviation safety community, sharing their experiences and insights with others affected by aviation accidents. They have formed support networks, ensuring that no one feels alone in their grief and struggle for justice.

While the pain of the Tenerife Airport Disaster's aftermath is enduring, the resilience and determination of survivors and the families of victims have left a lasting impact on the aviation industry. Their stories serve as a poignant reminder of the human toll of aviation accidents and inspire continuous efforts to improve safety and prevent similar tragedies in the future.

Amid the devastation of the Tenerife Airport Disaster, the tragedy holds a profound human touch, honoring the lives of those who were lost on that fateful day. Each passenger and crew member was more than a statistic; they were individuals with unique stories, dreams, and aspirations. In remembering them, we honor their memory and the impact they had on the lives of their loved ones.

Among the victims was a young couple, newly married and excitedly embarking on their honeymoon adventure. Their joy and laughter filled the air as they boarded the ill-fated flight, blissfully unaware of the events that lay ahead. Their families have cherished the memories of their smiles, their love for each other, and the dreams they had shared.

Another passenger, a veteran pilot, had spent decades soaring through the skies, finding tranquility in the clouds. He had mentored countless aviators, instilling in them a deep love for flying and a respect for the skies they navigated. His legacy lives on in the pilots he inspired, guiding their hands with his wisdom.

Among the crew members was a compassionate flight attendant, known for her warm heart and the way she cared for each passenger as if they were family. She had a knack for making strangers feel at ease, soothing their fears and brightening their journeys. Her kindness touched the lives of all who crossed her path.

And then there were the children, innocent souls whose laughter and curiosity had filled the cabins of those airplanes. Their future, brimming with potential, was tragically cut short. Each child represented hope, imagination, and the promise of tomorrow.

The families left behind have carried the weight of grief for decades, forever yearning for one more embrace, one more chance to say "I love you." Their loss has been immeasurable, and their hearts have been eternally scarred.

Yet, amidst the sorrow, the legacy of those lost endures. They are remembered in photographs, in stories shared, and in the hearts of their loved ones. Their lives, though tragically cut short, continue to inspire change and progress in the aviation industry, as their memory fuels the relentless pursuit of safer skies.

COLLISION COURSE: UNRAVELING THE TENERIFE AIRPORT DISASTER

In honoring those who perished in the Tenerife Airport Disaster, we are reminded of the fragility of life and the importance of cherishing every moment we have with our loved ones. Their memory serves as a poignant reminder that, in the face of tragedy, our collective humanity unites us, binding us together in a shared quest for a safer, more compassionate world. As we remember those who are no longer with us, we hold them close in our hearts, forever woven into the tapestry of the human experience. May their legacy be a beacon of hope, guiding us towards a future where safety, compassion, and remembrance coexist in harmony.

114

Chapter 16: Memorialization and Remembrance

In the wake of the Tenerife Airport Disaster, numerous memorials and tributes have been created to honor the victims and ensure that their memory lives on. These memorials serve as a poignant reminder of the tragedy and its impact on the aviation industry and the families of those who lost their lives. Here are some of the notable memorials and tributes dedicated to the victims:

1. Tenerife North Airport Memorial: At the site of the disaster, a memorial stands in remembrance of the victims. This solemn monument pays tribute to the lives lost on that tragic day and serves as a place of reflection and contemplation for visitors.

2. Remembrance Services: In the years following the accident, annual remembrance services have been held at Tenerife North Airport and other locations around the world. These services bring together survivors, families of the victims, aviation professionals, and community members to honor the memory of those who perished.

3. Pan Am Flight 1736 Memorial Park: In the United States, a memorial park was established in San Diego, California, dedicated to the victims of Pan Am Flight 1736. The park features a memorial wall with the names of the victims inscribed, providing a tranquil space for remembrance and reflection.

4. KLM Flight 4805 Memorial: In the Netherlands, a memorial site was created in the city of Amsterdam, paying tribute to the Dutch victims of KLM Flight 4805. The memorial provides a place for families and friends to gather and remember their loved ones.

5. Online Memorials and Websites: Various online memorials and websites have been created by families and organizations to share stories, photos, and memories of the victims. These virtual tributes allow people from around the world to pay their respects and learn more about the individuals who lost their lives.

6. Scholarships and Foundations: Several scholarships and foundations have been established in the names of the victims to support causes that were meaningful to them. These initiatives ensure that the legacies of the victims live on, making a positive impact in the areas they were passionate about.

7. Aviation Safety Initiatives: In honor of the victims, numerous aviation safety initiatives have been launched worldwide. These initiatives aim to promote continuous improvement in aviation safety and prevent similar accidents in the future.

8. Documentary Films and Books: Documentaries and books have been produced to chronicle the events of the Tenerife Airport Disaster and honor the memory of the victims. These storytelling mediums help preserve the history of the tragedy and its impact on aviation safety.

COLLISION COURSE: UNRAVELING THE TENERIFE AIRPORT DISASTER

The memorials and tributes dedicated to the victims of the Tenerife Airport Disaster serve as a powerful reminder of the human toll of aviation accidents and the importance of aviation safety. They offer solace and comfort to the families of the victims, while also educating the public about the significance of learning from past tragedies to prevent future ones. These memorials stand as symbols of resilience, unity, and a commitment to ensuring that the memory of those who lost their lives is never forgotten.

The importance of remembrance and learning from past tragedies cannot be overstated. Such remembrance serves as a testament to the lives lost and the profound impact of catastrophic events on individuals, families, communities, and society as a whole. Learning from past tragedies is essential to prevent similar incidents and make meaningful improvements in various aspects of life. Here are some reasons why remembrance and learning from past tragedies are crucial:

1. Honoring the Memory of the Victims: Remembrance is a way to honor the lives of those who lost their lives in tragic events. It allows us to recognize the individuality of each victim, their aspirations, and the impact they had on their loved ones' lives. Through remembrance, we show respect and empathy for the pain endured by the survivors and families of the victims.

2. Preserving History and Collective Memory: Past tragedies are part of our shared history, and remembering them ensures that future generations do not forget the lessons learned. It helps preserve the collective memory of our society and

informs younger generations about the challenges and triumphs of those who came before them.

3. Learning Opportunities: Tragedies often reveal vulnerabilities, mistakes, and shortcomings in systems and processes. By studying these events and understanding their causes, we gain valuable insights into how to prevent similar incidents in the future. Learning from the past allows us to identify risks and implement measures to enhance safety and security.

4. Improving Safety and Preparedness: Past tragedies provide valuable data and experience that can be used to enhance safety measures and emergency preparedness. This knowledge helps policymakers, regulators, and professionals in various industries make informed decisions and develop robust protocols to minimize risks and respond effectively to crises.

5. Fostering Empathy and Compassion: Remembrance cultivates empathy and compassion for those who have experienced loss and hardship. It encourages a sense of solidarity and community, prompting people to support one another in times of need.

6. Advocating for Change: Remembering past tragedies can inspire individuals and organizations to advocate for change and reforms. It encourages people to take action, advocate for improvements, and push for positive transformations in areas that have the potential to prevent future tragedies.

7. Strengthening Resilience: Learning from past tragedies helps societies and individuals build resilience. Understanding

the challenges and adversities faced by others allows us to prepare for potential risks and respond more effectively to unforeseen circumstances.

8. Promoting Accountability: Remembrance can prompt individuals and organizations to take responsibility for their actions and decisions. It encourages a culture of accountability, which is essential for maintaining integrity and preventing avoidable accidents or disasters.

Remembrance and learning from past tragedies are essential for creating a safer, more compassionate, and resilient world. By honoring the memory of those who have suffered, studying the causes and consequences of tragedies, and implementing necessary changes, we can work together to prevent future incidents and build a better future for generations to come. The collective commitment to remembering and learning from the past serves as a guiding light, ensuring that we continually strive to improve ourselves and the world we inhabit.

Chapter 17: Aviation Safety Today

The Tenerife Airport Disaster was a pivotal moment in aviation history that led to significant improvements in aviation safety. Since the tragic collision on March 27, 1977, the aviation industry has made remarkable strides to prevent similar incidents and enhance overall safety. Here is an analysis of the current state of aviation safety and the improvements made since the Tenerife disaster:

1. Safety Regulations and Standards: Aviation authorities worldwide have developed and enforced more stringent safety regulations and standards. These regulations cover a wide range of areas, including aircraft design, maintenance, crew training, air traffic management, and emergency response procedures.

2. Crew Resource Management (CRM): The adoption of CRM training has transformed the cockpit culture, emphasizing effective teamwork, communication, and decision-making among flight crews. This has contributed to a significant reduction in human error-related accidents.

3. Advanced Technology: The aviation industry has embraced technological advancements that have greatly improved safety. Modern aircraft are equipped with state-of-the-art avionics, collision avoidance systems, and weather radar, enhancing situational awareness and reducing the risk of accidents.

4. Improved Communication: Standardized communication protocols between air traffic control and flight crews have been implemented, reducing the likelihood of misunderstandings and miscommunications.

5. Weather Forecasting and Reporting: The accuracy and reliability of weather forecasting have greatly improved, enabling flight crews and air traffic controllers to make more informed decisions regarding adverse weather conditions.

6. Runway Safety Enhancements: Airports have implemented runway safety measures, such as improved signage, lighting, and markings, to reduce the risk of runway incursions and collisions.

7. Safety Reporting Systems: The establishment of voluntary safety reporting systems encourages aviation professionals to report safety concerns and near-miss incidents without fear of punitive actions. This has led to a better understanding of potential hazards and allowed for proactive risk mitigation.

8. Global Safety Initiatives: International organizations like the International Civil Aviation Organization (ICAO) have been instrumental in promoting global safety initiatives and setting safety standards that countries can adopt and implement.

9. Continuous Learning and Investigation: The aviation industry places a strong emphasis on continuous learning from accidents and incidents. Modern accident investigations use advanced techniques, including flight data analysis and simulation, to gain insights and improve safety measures.

10. Safety Culture: A strong safety culture permeates the aviation industry, emphasizing safety as the top priority for all stakeholders, including airlines, pilots, air traffic controllers, and maintenance personnel.

Overall, the current state of aviation safety reflects a transformation in the industry's approach to preventing accidents and improving safety standards. The lessons learned from the Tenerife Airport Disaster have been instrumental in driving these improvements. While the aviation industry has made significant progress, safety remains a continuous journey. Ongoing efforts to learn from past incidents, adopt new technologies, and refine safety protocols are essential to maintain the high standard of aviation safety achieved in the years since the Tenerife disaster. The commitment to a safer future continues to be a collective effort of all stakeholders in the aviation community.

Chapter 18: The Psychological Impact on Survivors and First Responders

The Tenerife Airport Disaster had a profound psychological impact on both survivors and first responders who witnessed and experienced the tragic events on March 27, 1977. The magnitude of the accident, with its immense loss of life and the catastrophic nature of the collision, left deep emotional scars on those directly involved in the rescue and recovery efforts. Here are some key aspects of the psychological impact on survivors and first responders:

Survivors:

1. Survivor's Guilt: Many survivors experienced survivor's guilt, a common psychological response where individuals feel guilt and a sense of unworthiness for having survived a tragedy when others did not. They may question why they were spared while others perished, leading to feelings of sadness and distress.

2. Trauma and PTSD: Survivors often suffered from post-traumatic stress disorder (PTSD) due to the traumatic experience they endured during the accident. The vivid and distressing memories of the collision, along with the sights, sounds, and smells of the wreckage, could lead to flashbacks, nightmares, and anxiety.

3. Emotional Distress: The survivors faced a range of emotions, including grief, fear, anger, and sadness. Coping with the emotional aftermath of the disaster was challenging, and some survivors needed professional counseling and support to process their feelings.

4. Fear of Flying: Many survivors developed a fear of flying or experienced heightened anxiety whenever they had to board an aircraft. The trauma of the accident made air travel a trigger for distressing memories and emotions.

First Responders:

1. Critical Incident Stress: First responders who were involved in the immediate aftermath of the disaster faced critical incident stress, a type of acute stress response resulting from exposure to traumatic events. Witnessing the loss of life and devastation could lead to psychological distress, including feelings of helplessness and grief.

2. Compassion Fatigue: First responders working tirelessly to rescue survivors and recover bodies from the wreckage could experience compassion fatigue, a form of emotional exhaustion resulting from prolonged exposure to the suffering of others.

3. Trauma Exposure and PTSD: The intense and emotionally charged nature of their work could expose first responders to secondary trauma, potentially leading to the development of PTSD symptoms.

4. Survivor's Guilt: In some cases, first responders might experience survivor's guilt if they were unable to save all the

victims. They might feel a sense of responsibility for the lives lost and struggle with feelings of inadequacy.

Support and Coping:

Both survivors and first responders benefited from professional support and counseling to cope with the psychological aftermath of the disaster. Crisis intervention teams and mental health professionals provided critical support to those directly affected by the tragedy. Peer support groups also played a significant role in helping survivors and first responders share their experiences, provide comfort, and validate their feelings.

In the years following the disaster, ongoing efforts were made to address the psychological needs of survivors, families of victims, and first responders. Recognition of the psychological impact of traumatic events has led to improved support systems and a greater awareness of the importance of mental health care in the aftermath of disasters.

It is essential to recognize that the psychological impact of a disaster of this magnitude is complex and multifaceted. Even decades later, survivors and first responders may continue to grapple with the effects of the tragedy. By acknowledging and addressing the psychological consequences, we can provide the necessary care and support to those affected, helping them on their journey of healing and recovery.

The importance of mental health support in the aftermath of catastrophic events like the Tenerife Airport Disaster cannot be overstated. Such incidents cause profound psychological trauma and distress for survivors, families of victims, and first responders. Mental health support is crucial in helping individuals cope with the emotional aftermath and promoting resilience and recovery. Here are several reasons why mental health support is essential in the aftermath of such events:

1. Addressing Trauma and PTSD: Traumatic events like the Tenerife Disaster can lead to post-traumatic stress disorder (PTSD) and other trauma-related disorders. Mental health support provides individuals with the necessary tools and coping mechanisms to process their experiences, reduce the impact of trauma, and facilitate healing.

2. Validating Emotions and Experiences: Individuals affected by such tragedies may experience a range of intense emotions, including grief, guilt, anxiety, and fear. Mental health professionals can validate these feelings, providing a safe space for individuals to express their emotions without judgment.

3. Reducing Stigma: Seeking mental health support after a disaster helps reduce the stigma surrounding mental health. It sends a message that it is okay to seek help and that mental well-being is a valid and essential aspect of overall health.

4. Preventing Long-Term Consequences: Untreated psychological trauma can lead to long-term consequences, affecting individuals' quality of life and functioning. Early intervention through mental health support can prevent the development of chronic mental health issues.

5. Facilitating Coping and Resilience: Mental health support equips individuals with coping strategies and resilience-building techniques to navigate the challenges they

face in the aftermath of the disaster. It empowers individuals to manage stress and adversity effectively.

6. Supporting Families and Communities: Disasters like the Tenerife Airport Collision affect not only individuals but entire families and communities. Mental health support fosters a sense of community care, helping people come together to heal and support one another.

7. Assisting First Responders: First responders are exposed to immense stress and trauma during and after the disaster. Mental health support is critical for their well-being, ensuring that they can continue their essential work while addressing their emotional needs.

8. Promoting Long-Term Recovery: Mental health support plays a significant role in the long-term recovery of those affected. It can help individuals gradually rebuild their lives and find meaning and purpose in the face of adversity.

9. Enhancing Coping Skills: Mental health professionals offer coping skills tailored to the unique experiences of survivors, families, and first responders. These skills can be invaluable in navigating challenges beyond the immediate aftermath of the disaster.

.10. Building Resilient Communities: By providing mental health support to individuals and communities affected by disasters, we contribute to building more resilient societies. Mental well-being is an integral aspect of community resilience.

Mental health support is a vital component of post-disaster care and recovery. It validates individuals' experiences, addresses trauma and mental health disorders, promotes coping and resilience, and fosters community care. Recognizing the importance of mental health in the aftermath of catastrophic events enables us to offer comprehensive support and care to those impacted, ultimately contributing to their healing and long-term well-being.

COLLISION COURSE: UNRAVELING THE TENERIFE AIRPORT DISASTER

Chapter 19: Other Notable Aviation Disasters and Lessons

1. Air France Flight 447 (2009):

On June 1, 2009, Air France Flight 447 crashed into the Atlantic Ocean during a flight from Rio de Janeiro, Brazil, to Paris, France, resulting in the loss of all 228 passengers and crew. The investigation revealed that the crash was caused by the malfunctioning of pitot tubes, which provided incorrect airspeed data to the flight computers. This incident highlighted the importance of proper instrument functioning and improved pilot training for handling critical situations, emphasizing manual flying skills in adverse conditions.

Lesson Learned: Ensuring accurate and reliable instruments and emphasizing manual flying proficiency for pilots are crucial for handling unexpected situations.

2. Malaysia Airlines Flight MH370 (2014):

On March 8, 2014, Malaysia Airlines Flight MH370 disappeared during a flight from Kuala Lumpur, Malaysia, to Beijing, China, with 239 people on board. The aircraft's whereabouts remain unknown, and the incident sparked a worldwide discussion about tracking and communication systems for commercial airliners. This tragedy led to a push for improved satellite-based tracking systems and real-time tracking of commercial flights.

Lesson Learned: Implementing more robust and continuous flight tracking systems is necessary to enhance aircraft location and improve response time in case of emergencies.

3. Germanwings Flight 9525 (2015):

On March 24, 2015, Germanwings Flight 9525 crashed in the French Alps, killing all 150 passengers and crew on board. The investigation determined that the co-pilot deliberately initiated the descent and crashed the plane intentionally. This incident raised concerns about pilot mental health and led to increased focus on psychological evaluations and support systems for pilots.

Lesson Learned: Ensuring comprehensive mental health evaluations for pilots and creating a supportive environment to address mental health concerns are crucial for flight safety.

4. Lion Air Flight 610 (2018):

On October 29, 2018, Lion Air Flight 610 crashed into the Java Sea shortly after takeoff from Jakarta, Indonesia, killing all 189 people on board. The investigation revealed that the crash was primarily caused by issues with the aircraft's Maneuvering Characteristics Augmentation System (MCAS). This tragedy shed light on the importance of pilot training and understanding new aircraft systems thoroughly.

Lesson Learned: Thorough pilot training on new systems and the importance of knowing how to handle malfunctions effectively are vital for safe flight operations.

5. Ethiopian Airlines Flight 302 (2019):

COLLISION COURSE: UNRAVELING THE TENERIFE AIRPORT DISASTER

On March 10, 2019, Ethiopian Airlines Flight 302 crashed shortly after takeoff from Addis Ababa, Ethiopia, killing all 157 passengers and crew. Similar to Lion Air Flight 610, the crash was attributed to issues with the MCAS system on the Boeing 737 MAX aircraft. This tragedy led to the worldwide grounding of the 737 MAX and an intense focus on aircraft design and certification processes.

Lesson Learned: Ensuring rigorous aircraft certification processes and proper training on new systems are critical for preventing accidents related to aircraft design flaws.

Each of these aviation disasters has provided valuable lessons that have driven improvements in aviation safety. From enhancing pilot training and mental health support to implementing better tracking and communication systems and emphasizing aircraft certification processes, the aviation industry continues to learn from past tragedies to create a safer and more secure future for air travel.

Chapter 20: Looking to the Future

As we conclude this book, it is evident that the Tenerife Airport Disaster, one of the deadliest aviation accidents in history, has left an indelible mark on the aviation industry. The tragedy served as a catalyst for a global commitment to enhance aviation safety and prevent similar incidents in the future. The lessons learned from this devastating event have driven continuous efforts to make air travel safer and more secure.

The aviation community has made remarkable strides in improving safety regulations, technology, training, and communication protocols. Crew resource management (CRM) training has transformed cockpit culture, promoting effective teamwork and decision-making among flight crews. Advanced technology, such as improved avionics and collision avoidance systems, has enhanced situational awareness and reduced the risk of accidents.

Air traffic control procedures have been optimized to enhance communication and reduce the likelihood of misunderstandings. The aviation industry's dedication to a robust safety culture has permeated all levels, fostering an environment where safety is paramount.

Crucial advancements in weather forecasting and reporting have allowed flight crews and air traffic controllers to navigate adverse weather conditions more effectively. Runway safety enhancements and continuous improvement in air traffic management contribute to safer ground operations.

The psychological impact of aviation disasters on survivors, families of victims, and first responders has also received increased attention. Mental health support has become an integral part of post-disaster care, ensuring that those affected receive the necessary help and support to cope with trauma and grief.

The tragic experiences of other significant aviation disasters, such as Air France Flight 447, Malaysia Airlines Flight MH370, Germanwings Flight 9525, Lion Air Flight 610, and Ethiopian Airlines Flight 302, have also contributed to a deeper understanding of potential risks and vulnerabilities in aviation operations.

Through the collaborative efforts of governments, aviation authorities, airlines, pilots, air traffic controllers, and industry experts, the aviation industry continues to strive for excellence in safety. Ongoing research, data analysis, and proactive measures are continuously implemented to stay ahead of emerging challenges and maintain the highest standards of safety.

The commitment to learning from past tragedies and preventing future ones is an ongoing journey, an unyielding dedication to preserving human lives and ensuring the well-being of air travelers worldwide.

As the final chapter of this book closes, let us remember the victims of the Tenerife Airport Disaster and all those who have lost their lives in aviation accidents. Their memory serves as a poignant reminder of the importance of our collective responsibility to create a safer, more secure aviation landscape. Together, we continue to build a future where aviation safety remains at the forefront, ensuring that the skies remain a symbol of hope, progress, and unity for generations to come.

The Tenerife Airport Disaster remains a haunting reminder of the devastating consequences that can arise from a combination of factors in the aviation industry. This tragic event has left an indelible mark on aviation history, reshaping the way we approach safety and demanding continuous improvements to prevent similar catastrophes in the future.

The collision between KLM Flight 4805 and Pan Am Flight 1736 serves as a poignant reminder of the critical importance of effective communication, crew resource management, and situational awareness in aviation operations. It highlights the significance of learning from past mistakes and tragedies to enhance safety protocols and prevent the recurrence of avoidable accidents.

Over the years, the aviation industry has made remarkable strides in implementing enhanced safety regulations, advanced technologies, and improved training methodologies. The enduring impact of the Tenerife Disaster can be seen in the evolution of a proactive safety culture that prioritizes the well-being of passengers, flight crews, and air traffic controllers alike.

The resilience of survivors, families of victims, and first responders has inspired a collective commitment to mental health support and care for those impacted by aviation disasters. The aviation community recognizes that addressing the psychological aftermath is integral to healing and fostering a stronger, more compassionate industry.

Moreover, the Tenerife Airport Disaster has contributed to the global conversation about aviation safety, inspiring cooperation and collaboration among nations and organizations. The tragedy transcends borders, uniting stakeholders worldwide in their dedication to creating a safer and more secure aviation landscape.

As we reflect on the Tenerife Airport Disaster, we must not forget the stories of those who lost their lives. Their memory serves as a constant reminder of the human toll of accidents and the responsibility we bear to honor their legacy through unwavering commitment to safety.

The enduring impact of this tragedy reverberates through the aviation industry and the world, shaping the way we approach safety, communication, training, and mental health support. It underscores the necessity of vigilance, continuous learning, and a deep sense of responsibility for the lives entrusted to aviation professionals.

Through ongoing efforts, collaboration, and a commitment to learning from the past, we honor the victims of the Tenerife Airport Disaster and all those who have lost their lives in aviation accidents. Their memory serves as a guiding light, propelling us toward a future where safety remains the cornerstone of air travel, and the skies stand as a symbol of hope, unity, and progress for generations to come.

141

Sign up to my free newsletter to get updates on new releases, FREE teaser chapters to upcoming releases and FREE digital short stories.

Or visit https://tinyurl.com/olanc

I never spam and you can unsubscribe at any time.

Don't miss out!

Visit the website below and you can sign up to receive emails whenever Oliver Lancaster publishes a new book. There's no charge and no obligation.

https://books2read.com/r/B-A-UNEZ-XGIMC

BOOKS 2 READ

Connecting independent readers to independent writers.

Also by Oliver Lancaster

Chernobyl: Unveiling the tragedy. A Comprehensive Account of the Nuclear Disaster

The Bhopal Gas Tragedy: Unraveling the Catastrophe of 1984

The Deepwater Horizon Oil Spill of 2010: A Disaster Unveiled

Fukushima Fallout: Unveiling the Truth behind the 2011 Nuclear Disaster

Minamata Disease: Poisoned Waters and the Battle for Justice (1932-1968)

Evil Women: Unmasking History's Most Notorious Women

Bundy The Dark Chronicles: America's Infamous Serial Killer

Dahmer The Dark Chronicles: America's Infamous Milwaukee Cannibal

Zodiac The Dark Chronicles: America's Infamous Cryptic Killer

Bigfoot: The Comprehensive Investigation into the Elusive Legend

Chasing Legends: The Truth behind the Chupacabra

Chasing Legends: The Truth behind the Loch Ness Monster

Aokigahara Forest: The Heartbreaking Secrets of Japan's Suicide Forest

The Amityville House: The Haunting Secrets of America's Most Infamous Residence

The Stanley Hotel: The Mystery of Colorado's Historic Landmark

The Tower of London: The Haunted Past and Secrets of Royal Ghosts

The Winchester Mystery House: The Riddle of Sarah Winchester's Mansion

Vanished Skies: The Mysterious Disappearance of Amelia Earhart

Vanishing Point: The Bermuda Triangle Exposed

Poveglia Island: Haunting Secrets of Italy's Most Terrifying Haunted Destination

Tracing Footsteps: The Mystery of Madeleine McCann

Inferno in the Sky: The Hindenburg Disaster

Challenger: Tragedy and Triumph - Unraveling the Space Shuttle Challenger Explosion

Collision Course: Unraveling The Tenerife Airport Disaster

Watch for more at https://tinyurl.com/olanc.

About the Author

Oliver Lancaster possesses an enchanting charm that effortlessly draws readers into the depths of his literary world. With an insatiable curiosity for the unexplained, he skillfully weaves tales of crime, conspiracy, mystery and the unknown, leaving readers on the edge of their seats.

Nestled away in the seclusion of his garden shed, Oliver finds solace and inspiration in the tranquility of nature. Surrounded by greenery and fragrant blooms, he dives into a realm of imagination, unearthing secrets that lie hidden within his mind.

Accompanying Oliver on his literary ventures is his faithful ginger cat named Italics. With his mesmerizing gaze and mysterious mannerisms, Italics adds an air of intrigue to Oliver's writing process, often curling up on a cushioned chair nearby, watching as words flow effortlessly from his human companion's pen.

When not engrossed in his craft, Oliver indulges in the gentle warmth of his garden with a glass of red wine.

Prepare to be spellbound as you delve into the pages of Oliver Lancaster's novels, for he is a master of the eerie, a weaver of secrets, and an unrivaled guide through the labyrinthine corridors of the human psyche.

Sign up to a free newsletter to get updates on new releases, FREE teaser chapters to upcoming releases and FREE digital short stories.

Read more at https://tinyurl.com/olanc.